China As I See It

By Pearl S. Buck

Pearl S. Buck

CHINA

As I See It

COMPILED AND EDITED BY
THEODORE F. HARRIS

The John Day Company

New York

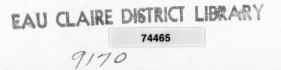

The John Day Company, 257 Park Avenue South, New York N.Y. 10010
an Intext publisher

Published on the same day in Canada by Longmans Canada Limited.

Library of Congress Catalogue Card Number: 79-107209
Printed in the United States of America
Designed by The Etheredges

Contents

Acknowledgment

I am grateful to the compiler and editor of this book, Theodore F. Harris, who is also my biographer. From a mass of unsorted manuscripts, piled on the shelves of the attic above my office, he has compiled and edited several books, of which this is the third to be published, the first being *To My Daughters, With Love* and the second *The Good Deed and Other Stories*. Other such compilations will follow in due course.

All the royalties and income from these books go to The Pearl S. Buck Foundation, an organization devoted to the welfare and education of Amerasians, who, born in Asia, are the children of American servicemen and Asian women.

Pearl S. Buck

Editor's Note

The pieces that make up this book, other than the final chapter which is newly written, are articles, speeches, and other papers about China I have selected from Pearl Buck's files of many years. Footnotes date and identify them to the best of my ability. If I have omitted to note that any piece included here was published in a certain periodical or delivered on a certain occasion, it is because of a gap in the files, for which I can only offer apologies.

Theodore F. Harris

Foreword

CHINA IS MORE than a part of me. She is in my heart and soul and mind. I was fed by her foods, I drank of her waters. Born in my own country, the United States of America, of pre-Revolutionary ancestry, it was China who nurtured me. My first conscious memories are of her people and her landscapes. They formed my childhood world, they shaped my adolescent years, they brought me to my maturity. I came in mid-life as a stranger to my own country and my own people. In some ways I am still a stranger here. I am foreign to much that is American.

It has been inevitable, therefore, that all through the years of exile from China I have continued to learn everything I could about the strange new life that is going on there; but the China that was mine and to which I belonged became Communist, and I knew I could no longer live there. I was forced to this conclusion because I very nearly lost my life at the hands of a Communist army which invaded the city where I lived. On that day I knew I was American, however Chinese I was in education and feeling.

Foreword

I have never returned to China since and it may be that I never shall. But I have kept my memories, my concern, my love. From time to time I have written of China and her people, in order that, hopefully, my American people could understand the Chinese better, as somehow we must. These papers have been gathered together in this book.

It will be seen that after 1951 I ceased abruptly to write on Chinese subjects. This was because no reliable information came to me from China. But I have continued to read, especially the writings of Europeans who could go to China, and while I myself have no direct correspondence with old friends there, I do hear from Chinese friends in the United States who are in desultory and secret correspondence with their relatives in China. Hence, in the concluding chapter I have written what I have been able to gather from such sources.

This book is timely, for soon we shall see changes in Chinese attitudes toward the outer world, or so I believe, and we must be ready. Even old tigers like Mao Tse-tung and Chiang Kai-shek cannot live forever. There is always a tomorrow.

Pearl S. Buck

January 26, 1970

China As I See It

1

The Land and the People of China

THESE TWO WORDS, *land* and *people*, are often linked together in the discussion of any particular group upon the earth's surface. They are used to mean *country*, the combination of nature and humanity, as distinct from the political entity contained in the word *nation*. So now I shall speak of China, land and people, and not of China as a nation.

Land and people anywhere shape each other. Land, I suppose, takes the first stroke. The land of China is vast and various. There are deserts in the north, and in the northwest high and barren mountains and close fertile valleys. There is frigid cold in the north; high bitter winds blow sand from still more distant deserts until the soil of the north is impregnated with sand. In the south the soil is deep and rich with the fullness of the tropics. The east faces the sea, and the west the Himalayas. Great rivers and lakes, high mountains, wide plains—everything that nature can

Speech, occasion uncertain, in 1948.

1

show is to be found in China. The finest fruits in the best variety are grown in China. From there have come plants which have enriched all the earth.

It was inevitable that this vast and various land should nourish a vast and various people. The Chinese have lived so long upon one piece of earth that they have developed a similarity of coloring which we in the United States will achieve only after many thousand years, if we are as successful as the Chinese in staying alive for so long. But aside from that, we find the land with its variety in foods nourishing very different-looking people. Those who live in the south eat rice as a staple, and they have in their origin, certainly in some places, a mixture of blood with aborigines, and they are shorter in stature than the people of the north. In feature they are more rugged, and in their character more energetic and more industrious, perhaps.

The people of the north eat wheat as a staple food, and they grow tall and strong. They are calm in temper, and it is commonly said that all the great Chinese philosophers and scholars have been men of the north. Diet, we know, shapes very much the stature and bone formation of any people, and over so long a period as China has lived, certainly her people show the variety of food. It is the more easily seen, for communications have still not developed very far beyond the foot and slow vehicle stages, and communities, until the present century, remained isolated, in large part. Provinces were as large and much larger than countries in Europe, and it was easy to live for generations content with the variety within a single province or even county. To this day, the average Chinese will reply, when you ask him where his home is, with the name of his ancestral village or city, in some distant province, rather than with the name of the city or place where he actually lives and works. The sense of belonging to a particular piece of earth is deep in the heart of every Chinese. He does not conceive of loyalty as adherence to a government, but to the very soil of his country and all that has sprung from that soil.

Yet all these people of China are unified. The essential unity of China is not in its political life, which has not until the present generation been of great importance. China's unity, so much more profound than our own, consists in its people's coherence as Chinese, the unity of a people who has lived in one part of the world for thousands of years, a unity of history and of habit. To such a people, accustomed to so profound a unity, the mere unity of a transient government means little. They are all Chinese, and that is enough.

Here in the United States ours is a political democracy. It is necessary that we Americans be closely knit together by government, for we are in so many other ways disunited. Our ancestry comes from every country under heaven, and we have no common history. Our languages are many. English is our *lingua franca*—a tongue borrowed from another people. Our minds are many, too, and our ways of living as various as the houses we build. In China the same people have lived together so long that they have actually learned what sort of house best suits them to live in, and whatever Chinese house you enter, unless it is a modern

3

house affected by the West, you will find the rooms laid out in somewhat the same manner. In the more formal rooms even the furniture will be so arranged that each person will know where it is proper for him to sit in relation to other persons in the family. Chinese architecture is as distinctive as that of ancient Greece, and it has modified itself to meet the topography—the high plains and slowly curving mountains of the north, the deep valleys and abrupt hills of the south.

Chinese democracy was built not in halls where victorious officers and leaders of the people met together to build a government for the people. Chinese democracy was built by the people themselves, living upon the land. It is the democracy of the family, paternalistic in its leadership, maternal in its responsibility for the welfare of every least member of the great family, ancient and established. This democracy exists today, ignored perhaps, but still alive and waiting to be recognized.

When Chinese modern democracy develops it will be in its own form, not like that of the Americans, but within its form it will contain the opportunities necessary for the life, liberty, and pursuit of happiness which all peoples crave.

Within the Chinese people, however, there are certain obstacles to this development. It would be unrealistic to deny them or to pretend that they do not exist. In this singularly united people there are deep divisions, traditional ones, which must be mended before a modern democratic life for China's people can begin to function. These divisions were less serious in old times, when they were better understood and guarded against. Now the old securities are gone. The emperor, for example, while he was revered as a heaven-appointed ruler, could be sharply criticized if he did not rule the people well, or if the price of rice went too high for common folk. Good ministers often risked their lives, in every dynasty, to stir to activity the conscience of a ruler, and the ministers were first themselves stirred by the protests of the people in streets and highways. Good governors were constantly renewed from among the most intelligent of the people by means of Imperial Examinations which, however they were defeated by occasional forms of graft, did search out from among the people those minds which were most capable of thought. Anyone could go up for examination, if he were sufficiently educated, and education could be found anywhere for the unusual individual, however humble his parentage. Honors and titles were not hereditary, moreover, as they were and are in England.

With democracy so profound and so essential, what then has kept China's people from developing more quickly a modern and working democracy which would give to the people voice of their own?

Foremost I should put the intellectuals of modern China and their remoteness from their own people. The traditional separation between the educated and uneducated Chinese individual was tragically wide even in modern times. In theory, in old times, the scholar was respected and even

5

revered by common folk, and at the same time he maintained a humble sense of responsibility toward the folk. He knew more, therefore he must exert his wisdom for the benefit of the people. This he often did. But he could also become haughty and superior. He could grow fingernails inches long to show that he did not concern himself with common toil—that, in brief, he was too good to work.

This haughtiness and false sense of superiority gradually crystallized into a sense of class, so that although anybody could be educated, if he had the ability and the opportunity, and certainly birth did not limit him, yet once an individual felt he was educated he could become an intellectual in the worst sense. China's modern intellectuals did not understand the native democracy of their own country. They did not, when they undertook to set up a republic, study their own land, their villages, their folk. They took their ideas from books, and from books of the West, and they tried to tailor a kind of foreign democracy which never came to life. I may even go so far as to say that too often these intellectuals did not value or even know their own people, except those in their own narrow circle.

The result of this traditionalism, this persistence of a false aristocracy, an intellectual class, is that the development of a new democracy in China, based upon the old, has been far too long delayed. The Chinese people are dependent upon their intellectuals. They need their articulateness, the facility, the knowledge, and techniques of the intellectuals.

But the contribution cannot be made unless these same intellectuals learn first from the people and discover there the foundation upon which to build the new China. A new structure must have a foundation. It cannot hang in the air and be sound and safe.

The second deep division in the Chinese people is between the rich and the poor. The sense of social responsibility in any rich man is very slight indeed. Religion working in Rockefellers made them give great gifts for the welfare of mankind, and similarly, religion working in Chinese rich men has moved them to build temples and shelters and rice kitchens—but not enough, in either case, to satisfy fundamental need or raise a structure. The average rich or even well-to-do person in China does not feel that poverty is his concern. I must say that I fear this will be the attitude, too, of the Western rich man as traditional religion releases its hold upon him. Alike in East and West, they eat, drink, and are merry. But the poor, wherever they are today, do not accept their poverty as once they did. They ask why they should starve while others feast. The question is being asked in China, too. The rich are uneasy and the division deepens.

The third division is between the official and the common man. This is a division little expressed in the United States, and where it is found it is kept secret. The common man is still strong here, thanks to early ideas of a practical democracy, and many as are the faults of our people, let it be said that the American official must still walk softly before the people. He must seem to obey the law, even if actually he does not do so. This is one of our virtues and let us acknowledge it!

But traditionally in China the official does not have to obey the law and the higher he is the less obligation he feels. The laws are made by officials for the people. Even speed laws are often not obeyed by officials. The theory is that an official is so good that he does not need laws. Actually he is no better than anybody else and so he breaks laws as he wishes and by doing so he sets himself apart from the people.

Such tradition must be changed. Intellectuals cannot hold themselves aloof as a separate and self-styled superior group; rich people must consider their obligations to those who starve and suffer; officials must think of themselves as servants of the people rather than as law-exempt superiors. Only when these old traditions are gone can a modern democracy rise from the great and ancient democracy of China.

The Chinese people have been nurtured in the spirit of freedom and individualism. Born upon a vast land, rooted there, family by family, through centuries, they must now cut themselves off from their roots. The old roots must produce new flower and fruit. But they cannot do so while the new growth of modern times is being choked by tradition that ought now to be rejected.

To some of you I may seem to have been somewhat political, after all, but I deny the charge. I have not discussed Communism and Nationalism. I have not compared governments. I have not told you that Chinese Communists are only "agrarian reformers." I have not talked about politics because I do not consider it fundamental to China's people. What I have tried to express is my profound belief in the Chinese, in the solidity and the unity of their life, and the reason why I think they are ready to become a modern democratic nation, while telling you why I think three specific traditions are holding back their rapid development in that direction.

I close by saying that I have absolute confidence in the Chinese. They have lived long and they have weathered everything long ago, even Communism. They exist, though their contemporaries in Greece and Rome have gone. They do not believe in aggressive war because they have too much common sense. They live, and have lived longer than any people have ever lived, with the possible exception of the people of India. They are not weak, they are not decadent. China's people upon the land are strong and resilient and practical. Nothing can destroy them. Only folly can ignore them, only stupidity and ignorance can despise them. They are sore beset by present trials but they are wending their way through them with ancient skill. They believe in their destiny, because they have lived so long that they know their destiny with all the sense of proportion which is their greatest wisdom. Knowing them, I too believe in this destiny and I know that it is a great one.

2

Interpretation of China to the West

I FEEL SOMEWHAT guilty in speaking on such a subject as the interpretation of China to the West, and for
two reasons: in the first place, I am not a professional
interpreter of anything to anybody, and in the second
place, I doubt very much the whole matter of interpretation.

I am, I say, not a professional interpreter—certainly not
of China. I dislike very much ever to have people call me
an interpreter of China. I am a novelist, pure and certainly
very simple, without the slightest sense of mission or obligation to anyone of any country. When people ask me, "Is this
true of China, do the Chinese say this, are the Chinese
that?" I can only answer, "I don't know—perhaps they do
somewhere in China. I have only seen it thus. But China is
a very huge country, full of many diverse persons and customs. I cannot pretend to speak for China or for anyone

*Talk at International House, Columbia University, New York City,
March 13, 1933.*

except myself. I cannot even pretend to interpret fully what I have seen myself. I can only portray, in my novelist's fashion, a few people I think are true. That they happen to be Chinese is because of the accident that put my life in China instead of in America or some other country. I am interested in the human heart and its behavior, not in the human heart of any particular country."

So you see, I am not well qualified to speak on the subject assigned to me.

Moreover, I doubt the whole question of the possibility of interpretation. Interpretation is limited by two things— the person who gives the interpretation, and the person who receives it. When anyone, Chinese or not, presumes to give his interpretation of China, and begins to lay down authoritatively certain rules and principles, I smile.

In a country so vast and so varying as China, where the average person travels comparatively little he cannot be blamed for not knowing many things even about his own country. He can and should be blamed as soon as possible for saying and thinking he knows everything. The interpreter, therefore, is limited by his experience, for however wide that experience is, it can at best be only the experience of one person with only one lifetime. He is further limited by his point of view, by his particular sense of mission. He may, for instance, be limited by a narrow definition of patriotism which compels him to reveal only what he considers favorable to his country, although in so doing he may be hiding admirable things. He may be limited, as many missionaries are, by the desire to get funds for some chari-

11

table cause and so reveal poorer and more pitiable aspects of life than are generally true. These are the best of motives in both cases.

The point is that no one person's interpretation of anything can be adequate or entirely correct, nor even one group's interpretations. The only possible approach to accuracy is in gathering together all interpretations and trying to find out what few points are common and what the significances are of the diversities.

But this is only to speak of the interpreter. The person who receives the interpretation must be considered also. He also is limited by experience and by mentality. If he is an ignorant person, and I suppose in any country there are only about two percent of the people who are not fairly ignorant, he judges what he hears entirely by his own experience. What is foreign to him, what is new to him, seems barbarous and strange and dreadful. If one is to restrain oneself from writing anything which might offend this person's ideas of what is good and right, one would be reduced to writing inanities, which would be unfortunate, or to writing nothing at all—which, I grant, might have advantages. The point is one cannot consider what will impress others favorably or unfavorably in any interpretation of anything. The only rule for an interpreter, if one feels he must be an interpreter of something, is to tell faithfully what he has seen and what he thinks he knows, continually remembering and saying that he is only one person and that he is liable to error.

The truth is that we do not interpret as we think we do.

We write books, we make speeches, we criticize each other's interpretations with great vigor and bitterness, each feeling the other wrong in presenting the tail of the elephant when the trunk is the thing. Meanwhile the public, both reading and observing, is learning about the subject we are interpreting, not from what we say, but from what we are. How often have I seen this! I have seen it in China when Westerners were trying to impress their religion upon people. With much speaking, by prayers and sermons and schools they have tried to interpret their religion. But the only time it has been interpreted and understood has been when people observing these Westerners, knowing their lives and understanding their spirit, understood something at least of what they were trying to interpret. I have heard people say in China,"This foreign religion is no good. See what a bad temper the missionary has!" I have heard people say, "This foreign religion must be true and good. See how good the missionary is who preaches it, how kind!" This is the only interpretation. Similarly, in this country I have observed Chinese who are also in a sense missionaries, who are zealous for their country. I have heard people say, "Of course I know China is a wonderful country and has a wonderful culture and history, but I don't like Chinese just the same. The only Chinese I know looked so cold and proud and seemed secret and unfriendly." Or they say, "I like China. I knew a Chinese girl in school who was the sweetest thing—always so kind and friendly. Why, I felt she was just like us. I never thought her different at all. I've always liked the Chinese ever since."

So here is the only interpretation, I think, that you or I can make of our country—to *be* the best our country, our civilization, can produce, and be that under all circumstances, whether people are kind or unkind, understanding or not, appreciative or not. There is lack of appreciation in every country—I have been hated in China for being white; in this country people hate the Negro for being black.

But this *being*, of course, must be preceded by a very thorough *knowing*. We cannot express a thing without first being completely familiar with that thing. I am much impressed with the fact that many of the young Chinese with whom I come into contact in this country are not persons of wide experience in their own land. Most usually they come from foreignized schools and environments straight to schools here, and school life is not, of course, broad in scope anywhere, nor typical of ordinary life. After all, they have spent their lives, or much of their lives, in a few large port cities, where life is more cosmopolitan than Chinese. One cannot, of course, blame them for this, but one must take it into account in any valuation of their interpretations of their country. Most regrettable of all, however, at least to me, is the fact that upon their return to their country, these young, intelligent, highly trained men and women seem to prefer to stay in the circles of port or large city life, rather than go into the other parts of China. Town, village, and countryside, all those places where the masses of people live, are fairly crying aloud for doctors, teachers, social workers of every kind. To go into these regions equipped with modern methods and education would indeed give one the right to interpret something of what one saw.

Here then are the only qualifications I know for being an interpreter. They are two. First and foremost, a spirit of humility and of inquiry which keeps one constantly learning at every source, constantly distrustful of one's own knowledge and ability to interpret.

Second, the unalterable conviction that one conveys, that one interprets, far more of one's country and civilization by what one *is* than by what one says. Speech, writing, are important and may have influence, but they have influence only when they are pervaded by this spirit of humility, of all detachment in the cause of truth. An angry or partisan point of view, however sincere, falls short of its aim. It fails because, however good it is, people discern its weakness and know it is one-sided. Interpretation is only another name for understanding, and before we can interpret any people to any other, we must understand and appreciate the fundamental humanity of all.

3

China and the West

I

FIFTY YEARS AGO China was scarcely thought of as an important factor in the affairs of the world. The interest of the Occident in that great country was either sentimental or curious. A bit of old porcelain, a painted fan, stately old mandarin figures marching across a fire screen—these were precious and marvelous as coming from that mysterious land, China. Beyond this point, little was known and less cared about a country of four hundred million human beings, differing in no wise in the quality of their humanity from millions of others upon the globe; a country occupying one and a half times the number of square miles in the United States.

During the last quarter of a century, however, China has been gradually drawing to herself the attention of the world.

Speech before the American Academy of Political Science, Philadelphia, April 8, 1933. Footnotes added.

No longer is she a place merely of queer customs, pretty bric-a-brac, and ubiquitous laundrymen. She has achieved a place, if an unstable place, in the family of nations, and the chief question about her now, torn as she is with civil war and rent with conflicting ideals, is, what will she become, what will she do next? What have we to expect, what to fear, from this huge and unwieldy mass of humanity?

The modern student of affairs must needs prognosticate enough to answer this question in some fashion, because, for weal or woe, China will assuredly influence the progress of the world in the next century and perhaps even in the next half century. The necessity to face this question presses upon all those who believe that the civilization of the West must be maintained.

For China is no longer remote. She is at last knocking at the doors of the Occident, entering eagerly into the colleges and universities, examining critically all that she sees, seizing ideas which she thinks will be useful to her, and returning again to her own land to use her new knowledge in her own fashion. It is undoubtable that, as the inevitable future leader of Asia, and as a monumental force in herself with her unmeasured resources both human and material, she will exert a tremendous influence upon the future of the world.

There is, however, in the Occident a vast ignorance of China. Perhaps the greatest ignorance exists where it should least be, namely, in the United States and England. It has been the ignorance not of willfulness, but rather of pleasant indifference, tinged with a distinct sense of superiority and of being busy with greater affairs. The time has now come when such ignorance is neither intelligent nor expedient. Senator William H. Seward said in 1853: "Who does not see, then, that every year hereafter European thought, European activity, although actually growing in force, and European connections, although actually becoming more interesting, will nevertheless sink in importance, while the Pacific Ocean, its shores, its islands and the vast regions beyond will become the chief theater of events in the world's great hereafter."

And it must be particularly important and interesting to Americans to watch the progress of China; first, because it was largely due to America that China started her republican experiment; and second, because of the relative position of the two countries. It is unnecessary to recapitulate the importance of the Pacific Basin in world politics. It is a commonplace. The Washington Conference proved this when it showed the Powers were willing to submit their military and naval programs to its review. The two greatest nations bordering on the Pacific are China and America, and China is great as yet only in its potentialities. The safety of democracy in the world must of necessity be greatly influenced by whether China makes a success of her experiment in democracy. If she succeeds, Asia as a whole will turn to democracy. If she fails, and there is only an increasing disorder among the oriental peoples, serious conflicts among the nations must result. America must support in her foreign policies every move for progress toward the building of a permanent democracy in her next-door neighbor across the sea.

One word is necessary in regard to the attitude with which a study of any Chinese question should be approached. The attitude must of necessity be as unbiased in all respects as possible. Let us forget, for the present, country and race, and remember only that we are human beings dwelling together upon the earth, our common home. Two wise sayings may guide us. Five hundred years before Christ, Confucius said, "Around the four seas, all men are brothers." And Bertrand Russell in recent times has given the second thought, when speaking of the mission of Great Britain to China under the leadership of Lord Macartney in the reign of Ch'ien Lung (1735–1796). The proposals brought by Lord Macartney were answered with the utmost patience by the emperor, who in a message to King George treated him as though he might have been a little child. He makes excuse for the British king thus:

"I do not forget the lonely remoteness of your island, cut off from the world by intervening wastes of sea, nor do I overlook your excusable ignorance of the usages of our Celestial Empire. I have consequently commanded my ministers to enlighten your ambassadors on the subject and have ordered the departure of your mission."

Bertrand Russell says concerning this extraordinary document: "What I want to suggest is that no one understands China until this document has ceased to seem absurd."*

*The Problem of China by Bertrand Russell, p. 51.

It is with such an attitude of understanding that we must review the history of the contact of the two great civilizations existing together in modern times, the one a product of the times, the other a relic of the ages.

It will be necessary before observing the changes wrought in China by the Western impact to know at least in a cursory way what conditions were existent there when the first visitors from Europe reached the shores of southern China, in order that we may have a sound basis of contrast. Then it will be necessary to take up briefly the main events which took place in the establishing of the Occident in China and the particular part the United States had in these events.

II

What was China's earliest contact with the Occident through Europe, and what was then her state of civilization?

It is difficult to answer the question of the exact time in which these contacts were first made. There are evidences in old manuscripts that trade in silk with Greece and the Roman Empire was carried on with China (known as Ta-Chin) as early as the second century. The Emperor Marcus Aurelius sent envoys to Cochin China to open trade there. Greek influences touched China through India and again in the seventh century the Emperor Theodosius sent an ambassador to the Chinese court. From the very imperfect Chinese government records we learn that before the seventh century A.D. ambassadors were sent out from China to surrounding nations with a view to establishing commercial intercourse. But there is no evidence that the Graeco-Roman culture made any impression on China. In A.D. 624 the Nestorian Christians founded a small colony in northern China. Evidently they were comparatively short lived and were either destroyed or intermingled with the Chinese to such an extent as to lose their identity. Rumor has it that they attempted to adapt their religion so thoroughly to the Chinese mind that there was nothing distinctive left and that thus they merged more easily into the country they came to convert. Certainly no trace is left of them beyond the time-worn tablet which, in defaced letters, gives an account of their exploits.

China's first real, although slender, contact with Europe, beyond that of casual traders, was through Marco Polo, that wise and good man. Well would it have been if all future visitors to the Middle Kingdom had been as beneficent and kindly a friend as he! He dwelt in China seventeen years under the court of Kublai Khan, and always in the most amicable relations with the people.

It was in 1295 that Marco Polo wrote his book of travels, and astounded Europe with his tales of the mighty but unknown empire. And indeed, in 1300 the Chinese were probably the most civilized people in the world. They were intellectual, cultured, and had made almost a religion of courteous relationships and peace. It was the middle of the Yüan dynasty. China had been conquered by the Mongols and was already beginning to absorb her conquerers slowly. The capital by this time was definitely settled in Peking, and out of that place, as an influence of the

Mongols, began to come a distinct stimulus to the intellectual and artistic life of China. China's history has always run in dynastic periods opening with renewed strength and vigor and gradually declining into weakness and corruptness and downfall to rise again in a new dynasty. Thus, though the Mongols were a ruder people than the Chinese, the incoming of a more youthful and more vigorous conquering nation brought strength. This may be a possible explanation of the permanence of Chinese civilization, that it has constantly received new vigor from the incoming of other peoples who have repeatedly conquered China only to be swallowed up by the conquered.

But it was not the China of Marco Polo which our ancestors saw. It was the China of the Ming dynasty, immediately after, which is the early China we must know, bearing in mind, however, the fresh vigor which came to the Chinese through the Mongols just before.

The Portuguese were the first of the European peoples to come to China, and they came with a double purpose, to establish trade and to propagate their religion. Their first voyage was made in 1517, under Ferdinand Perez d'Andrada, but we are chiefly indebted to the writings of the Jesuit missionaries of the order of Jesus, founded by Loyola, for the first detailed accounts of China. Their landing happened in this wise. In 1564 López de Legazpe took possession of the Philippines, and the Spaniards about that time having helped the Chinese in a scuffle with some pirates, a temporary friendship was formed. When the Chinese admiral returned to China in 1577, he took with

him two Augustine fathers. They were favorably received
and others soon followed, first among whom were Fathers
Pisio, Roger, and Ricci. Ricci resided for many years at
the court of the emperor, giving the emperor the benefit of
his knowledge of astronomy and medicines and, a more
doubtful gift, showed him how to make new war weapons
and improve the old ones already in use. This was the beginning of the period of Jesuit influence in China, and we
have ample data from the writings of priests as to the condition of society in China at this time as seen by Westerners,
as well as those aspects stated from the point of view of the
Chinese in their own books.

It should be said in regard to these data given by the
Jesuits, however, that there are varying views of their authen-
ticity. The data vary widely, some depicting the Chinese
as a most moral and intelligent nation and others giving the
reverse view. Isaac Vossius credits the former stories, and
extols the Chinese as the wisest of mankind, saying that
their inventions have been by far the most valuable made
in the world. But others assert that the Chinese have no
idea of God or morality and that their metaphysics are not
to be compared to that of the ancient Greeks or even to
that of the Barbarians, and that their morality is confined
to trifling ceremonies. DePauw exhibits the most violent
prejudice against the Chinese, discrediting the information
of the missionaries as sentimental and using language which
is almost abusive about the great nation which he himself
never saw.

The good Abbé Grosier gently reminds him of this fact

in the introduction to his *General Description of China* and in the ensuing chapters gives perhaps as fair an estimate of the people as can be found.

As a matter of fact, the Chinese were at a high stage of civilization during the Ming dynasty, and had been civilized for at least three thousand years, which is as far back as the Chinese histories go with any degree of clarity whatever. One need only read the *Analects* of Confucius, the *Great Learnings,* or perhaps, most of all, the *Doctrine of the Mean,* to realize to what a lofty stage Chinese philosophical thought had already risen. The ancient Chinese civilization is well known to be based on the Confucian ethics, so much so that some Chinese statesmen have said that they needed no constitution beyond these ethics. Five hundred years before Christ, Confucius had already enunciated a form of the Golden Rule, or Rule of Reciprocity; he insisted upon the brotherhood of men: he gave certain wise rules concerning the education of youth; he established the five basic relationships of life; he gave maxims of government; he described the superior man. In a word, a system of ethics more nearly than any other approaching that of Christianity was already accepted and practiced with some faithfulness in China at the time of the Mings.

But Chinese society at the time of the Mings "was like a mighty boulder. From its unknown rockbed after separation and movement in rolling down the stream of ages of experience it took long ago the shape which it retains. In contrast, the younger European civilization is more like a piece of conglomerate rock in which many diverse elements have been forced or fused into something like unity. . . . Most of China has evolved from within."*

The size, solidarity, and unity of China's society was indeed a thing for the more mongrel Europe to marvel at. Her population was stupendous. There were five reasons for this: namely, the observation of a form of filial piety which made it imperative to have progeny; the infamy attached to the childless; early marriage; frequent adopting of children to keep the family from extinction; constant child-bearing on the part of wives; taxes levied almost exclusively on the land, which left practically free of tax the tradesmen and mechanics; the few sailors and travelers; and an almost total lack of the type of gallantry which produces public women.

The unifying force in this great mass of humanity was Confucianism, which collected into its system all the best of Chinese thought and ethics, forming them into an orderly whole. Perhaps no country in the world has had so completely formulated and representative a system of ethics; representative of the best in its history and thought and therefore highly suitable to the people of all classes who revered its tenets and attempted to follow out the principles laid down in the Sacred Books.

The most important unit in the Chinese society at the time of the Mings was the greater family or clan, which was comprised of all branches of a family. The whole life of

*China's Story. Griffis, pp. 11 and 23.

China centered around the family system, and it was from ancient time highly paternalistic, so much so that the emperor required the heads of families to maintain order within their clans, and it was these heads of the clan who recommended persons for official positions in the government proper. So many books have been written on the subject of the Chinese family that it seems unnecessary here to give a detailed account of its workings.

Suffice it to say that the government of China at the time of the Mings was based upon the same paternalistic idea as was the family system. In many cases it was a benevolent paternalism, and the emperor was supposed to bear the same relation to the people as the father bears to his children. He was, moreover, their representative before heaven, and was responsible for their behavior, as citizens of the Celestial Empire.*

The provinces each had their own governor, and these were responsible to the emperor for the peace and good conduct of the province. It was a remarkably democratic system, and there has never been a government where administration was more decentralized, each official being responsible to the one above him, while the local people had much latitude for self-government. The emperor constantly sought the advice of his officials, and their advice was shaped by the desires of the people.

The government was always by "rule of men" rather

*The Emperor Yu had so strong a sense of responsibility that he said: "Are the people cold? Then it is I who am the cause. Are they hungry? It is my fault. Do they commit any crime? I ought to consider myself the culprit." Quoted in *The History of China,* D. C. Boulger, Vol. I, p. 5.

than "rule of law," however, and the people were dependent wholly upon the benevolence of the ruler. There was no constitution beyond, as has been mentioned previously, the Confucian code of ethics, nor was there any restriction placed upon the emperor, beyond that of public opinion. Chinese emperors were human, and while each new dynasty began well, with strong reforms, gradually each succeeding emperor became more effete and incompetent until the people could no longer endure conditions, and the existing dynasty was overthrown. Confucius says: "When proper persons exist, proper administration is carried on. When they die, it stops." The one inalienable right of the Chinese people was the right to rebel, and by this weapon, they could control the governors to some extent. Chinese history might be called a history of twenty-four rebellions.

Economically, the Chinese were in a fairly good condition in the Ming dynasty. Industry was in the handicraft stage, and men took time to be artists, and to finish with beautiful care every detail of their productions. In the cities the industries were organized into guilds, and the traditional industrial life, which was wholly controlled by these guilds, was a very peaceful one.

From this brief résumé of conditions in China at the time of the Mings, when the first contacts with the Occident were made, the following generalizations may be noted.

First, China was undoubtedly in a high state of civilization when Occidentals first reached her shores in any numbers. Her social system was carefully thought out and functioning with remarkable efficiency, and while based upon autocratic ideas, contained the germs of democracy.

Second, she was prosperous economically, and although she had frequent famines, they were local, and she had an immense population for the most part adequately fed.

Third, her educational system, while distinctly autocratic and conventionalized, was yet curiously democratic. Anyone might go to school, and by passing competitive examinations, rise higher and higher in the social scale. Chinese history is full of stories of men who rose from lowly positions to places of power. Liu Pei, seller of straw sandals, became a ruler of the Three Kingdoms; the first Ming emperor was a mendicant monk, and so on.

Fourth, the nature of the Chinese was one of excessive pride and self-satisfaction. This is not to be marveled at, when they saw nothing in the aspects, actions, or attainments of their first visitors to make them think themselves outdistanced in any way. Even the religion of the foreigner they considered infinitely inferior.

It is amusing to note, however, in this connection, that the pride of the Europeans was equal to that of China with certainly no more cause, and indeed, a study of peoples convinces one that there is none more excessive in pride than another. The difference comes in the mode of expression. China expressed hers in a desire for isolation. In the eyes of the Chinese the Western nations have expressed theirs in a determination to be aggressive and force their civilization willy-nilly upon the Far East, calmly convinced that it is superior. A Portuguese traveler of 1577 writes of his farewell remarks to the emperor of China thus:

"Emmanuel [the king of Portugal] had the highest sense of the extraordinary worth and uncommon fidelity of [the Chinese emperor] and was desirous not only to call him but to treat him in every sense as a friend and ally. He accordingly presented [him] with a golden crown, assuring him of the friendship and protection of his Portuguese majesty who would defend him from all his enemies."

One can imagine the Chinese courtiers laughing heartily after the audience at this presumption on the part of a paltry European nation to the great and self-sufficient Middle Kingdom.

It seems at least as absurd as the document quoted earlier in reply to Lord Macartney's mission.

III

To this proud, ancient, and isolated country came in the year 1516 the first vessel flying a European flag. It sailed into the harbor of Canton and was favorably received. Trade was opened up on a small scale; immediately Portuguese settlements followed. But the Portuguese commander of the third fleet that came to China committed a brutal outrage on a Chinese; he was seized by the angry people, who beheaded him and massacred his men in Ningpo. The Portuguese were driven to Macao, where they were finally allowed to settle.

The Spaniards were the next Europeans to come to the Far East, and in 1543 they seized the Philippines, and after the temporary friendship mentioned previously with the Chinese, they turned against them on the flimsy excuse of suspecting them of plots and massacred them. It was at this time that the ubiquitous name "foreign devil" came into use, which has been used ever since to denote anyone from a country other than China.

After the Spaniards, came the first Dutch traders. They were two Hartman brothers, who, having obtained a chart of the seas, sailed from Texel in 1595 and after vainly trying to establish a factory in Canton were compelled to withdraw. The Dutch then tried to seize Amoy but were driven out and compelled to retire to Formosa. They have never played an important part in the affairs of China proper.

Russia first came into contact with China in the reign of K'ang-hsi (1661–1722). Prior to his reign an embassy had been sent to China from Russia with the purpose of opening up trade, but the embassy had been received as tribute bearers from an inferior nation. Later, in 1670, a Chinese mission went to Russia, but there were misunderstandings, owing to language difficulties chiefly, and finally war broke out, which continued desultorily from 1682 to 1686.

France, like Holland, failed to get a foothold on the mainland of China, and Germany, busily engaged in consolidating her own empire, did not enter the Far East until 1897. It has therefore been Great Britain and America who have had the most definite part in the Occidentalization.

It must be confessed that the history of these early contacts is marked by the most wicked treatment of the Chinese by the foreigners. The massacre of the Chinese in the Philippines by the Spaniards, although the commercial activity of these very Chinese was of the greatest value to the settlement, Pinto's plunder of the tombs of Chinese kings, the rape of women by the Portuguese near Ningpo, the forcible occupation of the Pescadores by the Dutch, the pugnacity and affrontery of certain French traders, the constant appeal to force, all these and many other such instances, ofttimes costing the lives of peaceful citizens, filled the Chinese with horror. One writer commented: "These characteristics of avarice, lawlessness, and love of power have been the leading traits in the Chinese estimate of foreigners from their first acquaintance with them, and the latter have done little to disabuse Orientals upon these points."

It is not to be wondered at that China soon began to decide that she did not want the foreign trade at such a cost of bloodshed. With her inherent love of peace, fostered by the Confucian ethics and established by the Buddhistic ideal of the sacredness of life, she regarded these Europeans as barbarians and savages.

Yet the initial attitude of the Chinese toward the foreigners was friendly, and during the Ming dynasty they were distinctly welcomed as traders. The Jesuits were even treated with honor at the court, and no fewer than one hundred and fourteen of the courtiers were said to have become Christians. The Chinese have always been inherently fair-minded and predisposed to view a newcomer with interest rather than hostility and to allow him a fair chance. When the noted sinologue Dr. Arthur Smith was asked to give in one word the most striking quality of the Chinese he replied "Reasonableness," and those who know the Chinese best must confess that he was right.

The supposed determination of China to refuse all entrance to foreigners is not the wholly unreasonable performance it has seemed to many prejudiced minds. There were three reasons for it. First, a genuine, natural, and rather naïve inclination to believe that nothing could be gained from such an intercourse, since China had all she needed. Second, a feeling that if China did not impose herself upon other nations, they should not impose themselves upon her. Lastly, early in the contact with other people she had eaten of the bitter fruit of experience and found that these foreigners did indeed bring no good, but only force and bloodshed. She saw in the rude traders nothing of culture or religion, and she valued her own culture more highly than any pecuniary advantages of trade.

Her kindest attentions, as has been said, were at first given to the Jesuit missionaries, whose education and culture, although different from her own, she appreciated, until she saw with astonishment that these Jesuit priests insisted on their converts being subject to the Pope, and at this idea of a nation within a nation the emperor took alarm and refused admittance thereafter of Jesuits to the courts. As a matter of fact, the Jesuits had become embroiled in a question of the proper translation into Chinese of the word *God,* and had fallen to quarreling among themselves, and this had completed the disillusionment of the Chinese.

Furthermore, the fact that few of the foreigners, and at first practically none of them, seemed to be able to learn the Chinese language, had no apparent capacity to understand

Chinese literature or principles of policy, had to all appearances no religious life beyond that of the priests, did not understand morality or etiquette, and had no pleasures beyond those brought about by money and sensuality, all these were added reasons why the foreigners should not be respected.

It is not surprising, therefore, that the Chinese formed an adverse opinion of their visitors, nor, as they are a people slow to change their minds, that they have continued to hold that opinion even to the present day.

Toward the end of the Ming dynasty that had welcomed the foreign traders, the inevitable signs of corruption began to creep in, and once more China was conquered and the dynasty overthrown, this time by the Manchus. The last of the Mings was overthrown and the Ch'ing dynasty in 1661, with K'ang-hsi as its first ruler, assumed the power in China. The conquest was a fairly peaceful one, and the majority of the Chinese knew no great change in the government of their lives. The Manchus allowed many of the administrative positions to be held by the Chinese, and the Chinese craftily urged the Manchus to have the places of honor and affluence, maintaining them thus in idleness for generations until they became so effete that the Chinese were practically independent and became altogether so when the dynasty was overthrown to form a republic in 1911. There were two famous and good emperors in this dynasty, K'ang-hsi and Ch'ien Lung.

The war with Russia previously mentioned broke out in

the reign of K'ang-hsi who asked the Dutch to intermediate. Peace was finally made by a Jesuit priest and the first treaty between a foreign nation and China was consummated in 1686.

By this time England was establishing a trade with China through the East India Company, which had a factory in Amoy and another in Canton. In 1685, K'ang-hsi had issued an edict opening all ports to foreign trade, but this was withdrawn in 1757, leaving Canton alone open. Queen Elizabeth had sent an embassy to China in 1596 but the ship was lost with all hands at sea. It was not until the reign of Ch'ien Lung (1735–1796) that the British mission under Lord Macartney was able to present its demands at the Peking court, which demands were courteously but firmly refused.

The Chinese now began to view with alarm an entirely different spirit among the foreigners. Instead of the servile attitude of the East India officers, who had been willing to make any outward concessions for the sake of trade, claims to self-respect were made. By 1830 there were private merchantmen from the Occident going to China who actually said that all foreign trade would have to be on an international basis. This was preposterous in the eyes of the Chinese.

Officials reported to Peking that a crisis was approaching and the result was an edict secretly sent out to the Chinese maritime provinces recommending them to strengthen and repair their fleets to be prepared for the time when they "would scour the seas and drive off all European vessels of war that might come." Thus prepared, China calmly awaited the year 1834,* outwardly encouraging the foreign trade, seeing what the British government did not, that a war was bound to come forth from the denial of China's absolute supremacy.

The much-mooted question of extraterritorial rights for foreigners was inextricably mingled with this change of attitude on the part of the Chinese. At first the traders had taken it for granted that the Chinese might prosecute as they pleased on their own soil any foreign offenders of their lives. Several foreigners were seized for different offenses, and some of them were strangled, among these a Portuguese seaman whose only offense was that he had accidentally shot a Chinese while firing a salute of honor to an official. But in 1821, when two Chinese were killed in a scuffle with the sailors of the British warship *Topay,* the commander made it evident that further recognition of the Chinese claims of jurisdiction was out of the question. No more foreigners were given to Chinese courts and in 1822 this became a principle. The Chinese authorities then realized that the claim of extraterritorial rights was merely a reflection of the deeper-seated claim of international rights, the granting of which would spell the end of China's sovereignty.

The next few decades saw China being forced open at the point of a sword. In 1834, the year which the Chinese authorities knew to be the year of hostility, the long dis-

*The year 1834 was an important one because in that year the charter of the East India Company expired, and the British government, acting under the influence of the free trade movement at that time, decided not to renew it, but to put the English trade directly under the supervision of the English government. For a full account, see *Anglo-Chinese Commerce and Diplomacy,* A. J. Sargent, pp. 40-43.

cussion concerning England's importation of opium began, ending in the breaking out of the First Opium War in 1840. It is impossible to go into the detail of this. It has been said that China merely chose the opium question as a chance to open hostilities, since it admitted of a great deal of dialectic, and since she was really raising quantities of opium herself already. However true this British point of view may be, it is true, too, that the Chinese have always resented foreign importation of opium, and to them opium was the sole cause of the war.

The immediate reason for the war probably was that China wished to curtail the foreign trade because of the scarcity of her silver, which was beginning to alarm her. Within eleven years nearly 60,000,000 taels of silver had been sent from the country, and should this continue China saw nothing but bankruptcy ahead. Commissioners were sent to Canton to stop the illicit opium trade but failed, and after manifold disturbances and misunderstandings between the Chinese and British authorities, war broke out. The British at once carried it into the Yangtze valley and forced the Chinese, who were ill prepared to meet Western military force, to retreat and then to surrender. A treaty was made in Hong Kong in 1842, the famous Treaty of Nanking. By this treaty, Canton, Amoy, Foochow, Ningpo, and Shanghai were opened to British residents and commerce and the island of Hong Kong given to Great Britain as an entrepôt; extraterritorial rights of British citizens were also established; tariff autonomy was removed from China and $21,-000,000 indemnity was demanded. This treaty was the first of a number of greedy demands upon China. Yet it was not wholly successful, being couched in rather too general terms, and on a pretext of an affront offered to two of their soldiers, the British again declared war in 1856 and the proceedings of the British plenipotentiaries at this time were so outrageous that they actually, though indirectly, brought about the defeat of the Palmerston government in the House of Commons at that time. The war was brought to an end with the Treaty of Tientsin in 1858. The Chinese had fought a hopeless battle with inferior weapons but with the utmost gallantry up to the very end, when the French joined the British, hoping to get some of the spoils. This treaty legalized the opium trade, guaranteed protection to missionaries, opened the interior to traveling under reasonable conditions and opened several new ports to trade. An indemnity of four million taels was exacted, and a stipulation was made that Christianity was to be tolerated and foreigners were to be allowed to reside in Peking.

But there was some trouble about the foreign envoys getting to Peking, and hostilities again broke out and this time were taken to Peking, from which place the emperor fled and the foreign forces destroyed his palace, the old Summer Palace, together with many beautiful objets d'art.

As if this were not embarrassment enough for the Chinese, the Taiping Rebellion broke out and one of the chief causes of this was the impact of the two civilizations, imperfectly understood. It was at first semi-Christian in intent, and was supposed to be a sort of crusade against idolatry. Its half-crazed leaders destroyed temples and idols and worshiped

"God." The ideals were soon lost and half of China was disordered and in bloodshed. In despair the Chinese turned to their enemies, the British, for help, and the famous "Chinese Gordon" succeeded, as everyone knows, in quieting the rebellion. The Chinese displayed the utmost appreciation for the noble qualities of Gordon, in spite of the fact that a war was being waged with Britain in his very time. Even the statesman Li Hung-chang capitulated to the simple and honorable character. If the early contacts could have all been made through such men, how differently might the pages of history read, both now and in the future!

The next few years marched along still to the tune of incessant warfare for China and increasing agony of mind for her rulers, which broke out into active hatred against the foreigners in the great Boxer Rebellion of 1900 under the empress dowager. The details of how she usurped the throne are unimportant for our purpose. Important is the fact that she, a narrow-minded conservative, usurped the throne from the more intelligent, progressive Kuang Hsü, and shaped the policies according to her spirit until they culminated in the rebellion. Several warnings were given, revealing the state of mind of the Chinese toward foreigners: Roman Catholic missionaries were massacred in Tientsin in 1870; the famous murder of Mr. Margery of the British Consular Service occurred in 1870; the massacre of the French priests in 1874; war broke out with France in 1874–1875, resulting in the permanent establishment of the French in Tonkin; the murder of the German missionaries in Shantung in 1900, and then finally the Boxer Uprising came in grim earnest.

IV

But what of America, as all the European nations had been thus fighting and trying to gain entrance into the inaccessible China? America's share in it may be briefly reviewed thus.

In August, 1784, the first ship bearing the American flag, the *Empress of Asia*, from New York, sailed into Canton. But America, being less aggressive and needing new trade less than the other nations, made no particular headway in China until the Treaty of Nanking. In 1843 Congress gave the President $40,000 to enable him to establish trade connections with China. On May 8, Caleb Cushing of Massachusetts was appointed with the title of Minister and Plenipotentiary and was given three ships for his mission. A better man than Cushing could scarcely have been chosen to represent the United States. He was courteous, cultured, thoroughly good and wise. He reached Macao in 1844 and negotiated with the Chinese officials, saying that the United States desired no territory and while she would like to be able to trade in all ports, she would be satisfied to trade in the five ports opened to Great Britain by the Treaty of Nanking. On July 3, 1844, a treaty was signed peacefully, giving America all the commercial and future representative rights which Great Britain had, including extraterritoriality. Thus easily did America gain by reasonableness and friendliness what the others had fought for with bloodshed. It may be said that she gained it because the others had fought.

Remembering the essentially reasonable and peaceful character of the Chinese, however, it is a question whether more might not have been gained by other nations had their approach not been through force.

A new treaty with America in 1858 opened the way for missionaries and granted religious freedom to Chinese Christians. Ten years later another treaty was signed in Washington with a Chinese embassy headed by a former American representative to China, Anson Burlingame, who "sought to substitute fair diplomatic action in China for force." This treaty especially prohibited the importation of Chinese coolies, or forced immigrants, who had already been brought in large numbers to the United States, practically as slaves, to build the Pacific railways. While this measure was taken primarily for antislavery reasons, there was underlying feeling against the Chinese as immigrants.

In 1894 it looked as though the European nations were ready to partition China, and America felt it necessary to take steps in behalf of China and for the protection of her own trade interests in that country. Germany in 1898 had seized Kiaochow, using as the pretext the murder of two missionaries, and other nations immediately followed her example. Russia seized Port Arthur and Talienwan; Great Britain, Weihaiwei and Mees Bay; Italy asserted the right to develop the port of Sanmen, and Japan succeeded in separating Korea from the jurisdiction of China.

On the possibility that America would not have her share in commerce with China, the President told the ambassadors at the courts of the various powers to ask for a declaration of the "Open Door in China." It is unnecessary to go into detail concerning this policy, which has become as famous as the Monroe Doctrine. Certainly it saved China at a crucial moment.

Secretary of State Hay in his celebrated circular of July 3, 1900, sums up excellently America's policy in these words:

"To seek a solution which may bring about permanent safety and peace to China, preserve Chinese territories and administrative entity, protect all rights guaranteed to friendly powers by treaties and international law and safeguard forever the principles of equal and impartial trade with all parts of the Chinese Empire."

During all this time the great ferment against foreigners had been going on in China. Outraged in every way, China made one last great effort to cast out the foreign intruders and in 1900 the Boxer Uprising broke out with its well-known details of horror directed especially against Christians, not primarily because they were Christians but because they were foreigners, and against the Chinese Christians because they were supposed to be foreign sympathizers.

Because of the way the Powers had used their missionaries to demand concessions from China, the Chinese looked upon the missionaries simply as the political forerunners of the foreign governments and concluded that their presence could only work toward the gradual disintegration of the country. It was impossible for them to regard it otherwise, for while the missionaries were preaching a gospel of goodwill and peace, their governments, under whose protection they were working, were using the most unfair forms of coercion and aggression.

It was at once necessary for the Powers to send relief expeditions to China and once more Secretary Hay saw the "potentialities of great seizures" as demands for reparation on the part of the European nations. Again he sent around a circular note, reiterating the policy of the "Open Door" in China. All of the nations disclaimed any idea of partitioning China; most of them admitted the "Open Door" and on this basis, relief expeditions proceeded to Peking. Although the foreign histories do not, for the most part, tell it, and although it is impossible to excuse the cruelty of the Boxers, still it is true that these expeditions were very cruel in entering Peking. The Germans in particular will long be remembered for their heartless cruelty to many innocent villagers whose only crime was that they were Chinese. Their desire, the Germans said, was to make themselves remembered with fear and terror wherever they went. Soldiers of all nations were guilty of looting ruthlessly and left no good impression of the "Christian nations" behind them.

The Chinese were once more forced to capitulate at the point of the sword and in 1901 they agreed to make expiatory punishments, and memorials; to pay heavy indemnities and to improve the facilities for communication with Peking both in the physical route and in the organization of the Foreign Office, or Wai-Chiao-pu. The Americans were perhaps the least obnoxious of the relief forces, and the United States decided to use her share of the indemnity money for the education of Chinese students in American universities, and this greatly changed the attitude of the Chinese for the better toward the Americans at that time.

A final treaty was made between America and China in 1903, perpetuating the immigration clause of 1894; opening up new ports and inland navigation; providing for mining rights, the protection of trademarks, and copyrights; providing for missions to rent and lease lands and buildings, and for Chinese converts to be freed from the obligation to support the old religions in which they did not believe. It was this treaty also which provided finally for the use of the indemnity money of 1900.

In 1899 Hay had further developed the policy of the Powers toward China by maintaining that the ports in the spheres of influence which every nation except America had marked out for herself, should be opened to trade from other countries; and in 1904, as the Russo-Japanese War was being waged, he asked Great Britain, France, and Germany to make Russia and Japan recognize the neutrality of China in the war and to respect her borders. In 1905 he again circulated a note hoping that "no Chinese territory would be conceded to neutral powers after the war," and in 1905 Roosevelt brought the war to a close. The Open Door was permanently open.

Meanwhile, the Boxer Uprising had had two results. Foreigners saw that all was not well in China, and that there was a deep undercurrent of hatred against them. This hatred extended somewhat even to the Americans, in spite of the indemnity, because in 1898 the United States, failing to obtain the concession she desired of the Peking-Hankow Railway, obtained the Canton-Hankow Railway. It was expressly stipulated in the Supplementary Agreement of 1900 that "the Americans cannot transfer the rights of this agreement to other nations or to the people of other nationalities." The American China Development Company, which had the concession, deliberately sold shares to the Belgians until they acquired a controlling interest in the line. The Chinese government protested in vain, and finally bought the railway back by borrowing money from Hong Kong. This affair had two bad results. First, it showed the Chinese that the United States had a selfish interest in China, and second, it appeared that she could not be trusted to keep her word. When in 1904 the United States claimed that an American syndicate had been granted the right to participate with the British in the Hankow-Szechuan line, Chang Chih-tung, remembering the previous experience, absolutely refused to admit the American interests.

The second result of the Boxer Uprising was that China realized at last that her civilization was inadequate for modern conditions. Indeed, China had cause to face her situation with dismay. Her civilization, however valuable and beautiful, was no longer useful. Her leaders, smarting under the disgrace of her humiliation to the foreign powers, faced everything and decided grimly that the only way to fight the West was to learn to use Western weapons and to understand the Western civilization, however inferior it might be in reality to their own. Previous to 1900 there were some men who had seen this. Chang Chih-tung had

written his remarkable book, *China's Only Hope,* epitomizing
the situation. It became evident after 1900 that radical reforms of some sort must be undertaken if the empire was
to survive. A few futile reforms that did not touch the pres-
tige and emoluments of the ruling Manchu dynasty were
attempted, and after 1905 a belated and reluctant reform
policy was actually started, chiefly made up of useless royal
edicts. It was insufficient to stem the rising tide of Chinese
national spirit. The Manchu empire fell, a tremendous stimulus to reform came into expression, and the leaders of the
reform movement decided with a simple and almost childlike naïveté, but with a sober realization of the necessity
for change, that they would have a republican form of
government. In 1911, upon the ruin of disorder and corrupt
administration and subjugation to foreign nations which the
Manchu dynasty had left as its legacy, the Republic of
China, the Chung-Hua Ming-Kuo, was established.

What of the Western nations and particularly America
during this time of change in China? In 1911 there was a
distinct tendency on the part of the Powers not to recognize
the new government. The Six Power Loan was in discussion
soon after, whereby the bankers of Great Britain, France,
Germany, Japan, Russia, and the United States were to
lend money to the new Chinese government. President
Wilson saw the political implications in this loan, especially
in the inclusion of Japan and Russia, who had no money
to lend. In 1913, therefore, he was the first to recognize
the Republic of China and at the same time to withdraw
from the Six Power Loan.

"The conditions of the loan," he said, "seem to us to touch very nearly the administration and independence of China herself and this administration does not feel that it ought, even by implication, to be a party to those conditions."

The other five nations continued, but the Chinese government was suspicious and the negotiation was indefinitely delayed.

It has been in the League of Nations that China has obtained her fairest recognition. Yet, even there they early felt themselves unfairly treated in the giving of Kiaochow to Japan and later in the refusal of the League to allow China to sit as one of the major powers, a refusal which threatened a temporary withdrawal of China.

But the Chinese themselves did not expect a great deal from the League of Nations. One of the delegates to the Peace Conference, when told that China must look to the League of Nations to redress the Shantung wrong, very acutely summed up the true situation in these points.

"The ruling force in any League constituted at this time will be the same major powers that composed the Council of Five at Paris and which made the decision in the Shantung question. It is not logical to assume that a League of Nations created by the same body as the treaty and in conjunction with the treaty is designed to reverse the terms of the treaty. It is only the so-called weak nations that are asked to depend for justice and security upon the League of Nations, while the so-called Powers openly decline to

46

risk their positions upon the League alone and plainly regard its assurances as insufficient."*

China's tariff situation was the subject of much discussion. Before the Washington Conference for the Limitation of Armaments, it was most unjust. She might make her own tariff only within exceedingly narrow limits and she could not discriminate between luxuries and necessities as imports; neither could she increase her duties for revenue purposes. She had practically to do as the other nations said.

At Washington she asked for certain steps to be granted which would lead to tariff autonomy. Japan was chiefly instrumental in preventing the assent to all but a small portion of what she wanted. The new Banking Consortium resulted, however. It was formed by banking groups in America, England, France, and Japan, and the chief importance of this organization was that it stated as the definite policy of the Powers that international cooperation and control would be maintained in China; this, of course, is nothing more nor less than a final retiteration of the "Open Door." It might have resulted in the internationalization of China's railways. Most of all it prevented further direct efforts on the part of Japan to get control of China. But the Consortium has never functioned, because it was fraught with too much danger in the minds of the Chinese from the beginning.

But the political facts of America's policy in China during

*China Awakened. Tyau, p. 328.

47

the last seven years are too well known to need recapitulation here. More interesting, perhaps, than such recapitulation of recent events is the matter of America's attitude toward China during these years. Diplomatically it has been steadily consistent and friendly, but only reservedly cooperative, not going, perhaps, beyond the bounds of detached friendliness. It is best exemplified in the situation today, which presents the spectacle of America's watching with puzzled concern and with real sympathy China's plight at the hands of Japan. Certainly American public opinion is with China, but this public opinion is not crystallized to the point of direct aid to China.

In fact, the greatest and perhaps only actual diplomatic aid which the United States has rendered to China has been in the Open Door Policy, that is, the refusal to recognize any agreement between China and other countries which impairs the rights of American citizens in China, and which does not recognize the political and territorial integrity of China.

It is a contribution, of course, of which Americans may well be proud, and yet, from the Chinese point of view it has not been completely beneficent. The Chinese realize that it has kept China integral. Yet, they say, the United States did not carry the policy to its utmost and prevent spheres of influence and the making of unjust treaties. Moreover, it is said, and with some justice, that the concern of the United States was for herself, that she has taken also all the benefits of the unequal treaties, and that the only reason she did not pursue the same aggression as the other nations was because she did not have their need, having within herself sufficient territory and trade for the time. The general conclusion, therefore, based on these criticisms, is that the Open Door Policy has been beneficial to China, yet negatively beneficial. Undoubtedly, however, this policy held in check the rapacity of other Powers at a time when China was weak and made the seizure of parts of China less profitable by compelling one nation to share the spoils with others.

But apart from diplomatic policy the attitude of the United States toward China has always been friendly. Private enterprise has financed the missionary movement and trade. The missionary movement is too large a matter to discuss here, but undoubtedly it has had its share in the friendly relations between China and the United States. If its influence upon the individual by the individual has not always been happy, to it must be given the credit for having hastened, at least, modern achievements in education and science, notably in medicine.

American trade with China has not been of greatest importance to either of the two countries as yet, and at present the trend is perhaps not toward any markedly greater development. China has in the most recent years turned to the League of Nations for her advisory experts instead of, as she once did, to the United States. This has inevitably resulted in an increase in European influence in China, which may well result in an increase of markets for Europe. Moreover, the Chinese themselves now definitely realize that they cannot look to the United States, as they once thought they could, for definite and practical help against their enemies. They know now that while America's policy is friendly toward China, it is negative, and for all positive action they must look to themselves.

This will inevitably result in the strengthening of the military party in China. Her army will be modernized, and for the next century she will put her main strength into making herself strong in army and navy. She has no other recourse, since none comes to her aid.

It is natural at this time, perhaps, that the United States maintains her negatively friendly attitude, feeling remote from China's problems and puzzled by their complexity. But this negativity may one day be fraught with gravest danger for the world, when China, with all her millions, wakes late to the knowledge of the power of arms and imperialism.

4

The Young Chinese Discover China

ONE OF THE MOST important movements in China today is the discovery of their own country by young Chinese intellectuals. A generation ago the most progressive of their fathers were beginning to feel a stirring discontent with their own country. They were conscious, indeed the consciousness was forced upon them, that China as she had been in the past was not able to meet the dangerous and aggressive modernity of the West. I do not mean the political modernity so much as the march of economic, educational, and scientific events, which may or may not result in political and military events. These Chinese fathers of the present generation in China were the real revolutionists. They forced out of existence the old dynastic system; they changed with incredible speed the system of education; with indefatigable zeal they planned and set up a scheme of modern government. No ancient government under an emperor ever accomplished with more imperial speed such tremendous changes in so great a country.

Speech, occasion uncertain, in 1935.

In this atmosphere of change, of idealization of things modern and therefore Western and foreign, the present youth of China has grown up. Where the fathers imbibed the doctrines of Confucius and learned the classics and revolted against them these young people have been battered by many forces of the new times. They have been taught something of science, something of Christianity, something of atheism, something of free love, something of Communists, something of Western philosophy, something of modern militarism, something, in fact, of everything. In the sturdy medievalism of the masses of their countrymen the young intellectuals have been taught the most extreme of every culture. Intellectually they have been forced to the same great omissions that China has made physically. They have skipped, figuratively speaking, from the period of the unimproved country road to the airplane era. The omission was too great. The mind could not compensate for it. The spirit was lost in the conflict.

The first result, therefore, of the hiatus was undoubtedly to produce a class of young Chinese, both men and women, but chiefly men, who frankly did not know how to live in their own country or in the age in which their country still was. They were for the most part educated abroad, where they forgot the realities of their own race. It was easy enough for various revolutionary leaders to persuade these alienated minds that China's so-called backwardness was due primarily to political and material interference by foreign powers. The world was made the scapegoat for China's medievalism. Instead of realizing that China was in her own way making her own steps, slowly, it is true, and somewhat ponderously, toward modernity, it was easy hue and cry to say that if it had not been for foreigners, she would have been already on an equality, in material terms, with other nations.

The result of this was a fresh revolution of a sort. China practically rid herself of her two great grievances outside of Japan, extraterritoriality and the tariff. No visible change appeared as a consequence. It became apparent that what had been weaknesses were still weaknesses, and that these were inherent in the ideology of the people. It was found, for instance, that when a revolutionary leader became secure and entrenched he became conservative and too often as corrupt as an old-style official. The same has been true in other histories. There were too many honest and intelligent young minds in China not to observe and accept the truth, that the outside world had very little to do with China's condition, and what it had to do with it could have been prevented if China had been less self-satisfied earlier and her leaders less blind and selfish.

Then followed a period of despair and frenzy and increased idealization of the West. The evident prosperity of foreign countries was felt to be a direct fruit of Western scientific development. It was a time when the inferiority complex was rampant in China, and the young patriot was divided between mortification at what his country was and desire to conceal it from foreigners. There was no truth to be found in them, so far as their own country was concerned, and they at once hated and admired the foreigners.

What would have happened if the West had continued prosperous and at peace cannot be said. It is enough that the West did not so continue. The Chinese have viewed with interest and considerable satisfaction the Great Depression, the breakdown of prosperity, and the failure of scientific men to prevent depression. They have begun to say to themselves that after all China is not so bad. Evidently there is hunger everywhere, there are bandits everywhere, and one people is not better than another, and if this is so, then perhaps China was right in olden times, and perhaps it is just as well to go back and see what the old Chinese philosophy was. At least it taught people to live with contentment and some enjoyment of small things if they had not the great ones, and it regulated life and provided a certain amount of security and safety. The recent interest in China on the part of the West, the wistfulness of certain Western persons who envy the simplicity of China's primitive life and admire her arts and philosophy have also helped to inspire the young Chinese with some confidence in himself.

The result today is simply a reiteration of the old Biblical adage that the fathers have eaten sour grapes and the children's teeth are set on edge. Young China, wearied of the revolutionary ardors of its fathers, is going back to old China. It is almost amusing to see the self-conscious determination to be really Chinese, to eat only Chinese food, to live in Chinese ways, to dress in Chinese clothes. It is as much of a fad and a pose to be entirely Chinese these days, among certain young Westernized Chinese in China, as it was for their fathers to wear foreign clothes and eat with knives and forks and want to go to Harvard. These present young people have worn foreign clothes all their lives and eaten foreign food and they did go to Harvard, and they know English literature infinitely better than their own, and now they are sick of it all and want to go back to their grandfathers.

The trend is apparent everywhere, and not only in the externals of dress and customs. Far more importantly is it to be seen in art and literature. The subjects of modern Chinese novels of a few years ago, for instance, dealt chiefly with modern love situations, with semiforeign liaisons, with rebellions against home and parents, and the whole tone was somewhat sickly and certainly totally unrooted in the country. There is still more than enough of this in both art and literature, but health is beginning to creep in, the health of life from plain people living plain and sturdy lives. The young intellectuals are beginning to discover their own masses. They are beginning to find that life in the countryside, in small towns and villages is the real and native life of China, fortunately still fairly untouched with the mixed modernism which has made their own lives unhealthy. They are beginning to feel themselves happy that there is this great solid foundation in their nation, and to turn to it eagerly for fresh inspiration. It is new to them, it is delightful, it is humorous, it is worth having; above all, it is purely Chinese.

They have been helped to this new viewpoint, too. They would not, I think, have achieved it so well alone, and it is the West which has helped them. We of the West have helped them not only negatively, by exhibiting a certain sort of breakdown in our own civilization, but we have helped them positively by our own trend toward elemental life. The Western interest in all proletarian movements has sent young China to think about her own proletariat, and to discover the extraordinary quality of her own country people, maintaining their own life pure and incredibly undisturbed by the world's confusion. It is natural that this tranquillity should greatly appeal to them in their own confusion and sense of being lost in the twisted times.

Communism, too, has helped them. Communism has brought about class consciousness, it has made the common man articulate and demanding, and since modern education in China has been available to the children of common people, they have early been given a sort of voice, at least, wherewith to speak for themselves, however inadequately. In the art and literature of the young Leftists in China there is a rapidly spreading perception of the value of the common man and woman of the country. The expression is still crude and too influenced by foreign art, but the notion is there. One sees a peasant woman upon a canvas instead of a bird upon a bamboo twig, and the thick, straining figures of men pushing wheelbarrows instead of goldfish swimming in a lotus pool. This is hopeful.

Yes, young China now is upon the right road. To delve into the vital treasures of their own immeasurable past with brains sharpened by modern perceptions is to have an extraordinary opportunity these days. Young China is lucky!

5

East and West—Are We Different?

O<small>NE OF THE SIMILARITIES</small> between Orient and and Occident is soon obvious and it is that we take for granted that we are different. I have found it as astonishing to the Westerner when he hears that the Chinese eats bread and meat and cabbage, as it is to the Chinese when he hears that the American also eats rice and beans and shrimps. It is apparently far easier for the American to believe that the Chinese eats rats and mice and snakes and far easier for the Chinese to believe that the American likes his meat raw and that he tears it apart with pronged and bladed instruments. I have stood beside an old Chinese farmer at a railroad crossing in a Chinese countryside, waiting for the train to go by, and had him turn to me with pride as the train thundered by his wheelbarrow and say, "Of course you don't see anything like that in your country," and I

Speech before the Institute of Public Affairs, Charlottesville, Virginia, July 8, 1935.

have had an American farmer, upon hearing of my origin, say with complacency, "I reckon you travel by camels and sedans and the like over there. I suppose the trains ain't got so far as China."

We cannot believe that we are not different. Difference in skin and hair and stature convinces us that there is difference in more fundamental ways. I suppose few Western mothers who have lived on terms of friendship with Chinese mothers have not had the question asked them, "Tell me, I hear that you do not conceive and bear children as we do. How then do you give birth?" They cannot believe that sex is differentiated in the West as it is in the East. I suppose to them our women seem large and masculine in appearance, just as we in America love to say, "In China the men wear skirts and the women wear trousers." One generalization is true in about the same measure as the other.

The truth is, of course, that we like to think we are different. We like it because we like to hear of strange things, and because we enjoy the feeling of superiority it gives us when we hear that others do not have what we have, or that they do not know how to do what we do. East or West, the same look of incredulity and disappointment comes over the face of the questioner when he is given the answer, "Oh, they are very much like us—people are about the same anywhere." Something romantic, something fabulous, is gone, and we all love the romantic and the fabulous. And so how alike we are! We even make our

58

villains the same way—that is, we make them as different as possible from ourselves. The villain in the American popular novel and movie is sly and dark and Oriental, and he deals in drugs and opium, and he has a dreadful dark smooth cultivated wickedness. The villain in the Chinese popular novel or movie is tall and blue-eyed and high-nosed, with fuzzy red hair, Anglo-Saxon stature and Anglo-Saxon complexion. He roars and rants and eats huge amounts of meats, and is altogether a fearful and barbarous creature. Even in the Chinese novels of centuries ago the villains were blue-eyed and red-bearded and their noses were measured by the span. But the principle of selection is the same. The villain is, in short, always the other fellow.

And that is what we like to believe. We like to believe, of course, that what we do is the right and civilized way and all other ways are wrong or barbarous, or at best simply amusing, and we tolerate such things because we are amused—and when I say "we," I do not mean we of the West, but I mean us all, East and West.

Therefore, I shall not today waste time on the many and minor differences between East and West. Differences of food and dress, of house and home, even of language, are not in themselves important or significant. They are entirely the result of experience in living, and of choice, and bear the same relation to essential nature as does the fact that one person may prefer yellow and another green. That there are these preferences is interesting and may be significant provided one goes back far enough into the reasons which prompt such choice, although the differences in themselves are not important. What I propose to do instead is to penetrate, as far as I am able in this hour, into the real reasons for difference and likeness between East and West. But before I go on, I shall explain that I shall take as types the Chinese of the Orient and the American of the Occident. The reason for this is of course obvious. Aside from the fact that I am personally most familiar with these two sides of the world, it may be fairly reasoned that they bear about the same proportional relation to their hemispheres. There are many Oriental peoples, each differing somewhat from the other, so that we cannot say that or that one is the real Oriental. Occidentals differ as widely. The Englishman, the modern man of Sweden or of France, certainly differ from each other, and yet if we were compelled to classify, we would put the Hindus, Japanese, and Chinese into one Oriental group and the American and the Englishman and the Swede and the Frenchman into the other Occidental group. But the demarcation is not so clear as I seem to make it. Between the extremes are an infinite number of graduated peoples and individuals where we find influences of East and West indistinguishably mingled. The Orientalized Occidental, the Occidentalized Oriental, are obvious, but there are other similar influences between East and West more subtle than these—influences of schools, of religions, of trade, of travel, of books, of hearsay, so that gradually East is creeping into West and West into East. You would be amazed, I am sure, unless you know it already, if I were to tell you all the influences I find here in the United States of Japan and China and India, and even of Muslim countries. It makes some interesting thought. But again these are individual likenesses, and not more important therefore than the individual differences.

Quite arbitrarily, therefore, choosing as my types American and Chinese, I shall proceed to my first broad generalization, which is probably no more true than most generalizations, but one has to make some sort of foundation. I shall say that what seems to me the greatest difference between Orient and Occident is that they are logically unlike, and what seems to be their greatest similarity is that they are emotionally alike. That is, we *think* differently and we *feel* the same. All differences in external ways are the result of this difference in thinking and of this similarity in feeling. Let me illustrate very simply. If you gave a Chinese artist and an American artist the same materials and told each to paint a picture portraying the same obvious subject, the result would of course be entirely different. The feeling in both would be the same, provided the subject were simple and obvious enough, but the idea behind the emotion—the mental conception—would be different, and usually so different that to the casual observer the emotion would also seem to be different, although it would not truly be so. Take, for instance, a few further concrete examples. An American son would leap into the water to save a stranger, without thought, probably, of his parents. Indeed his parents would be proud of him, and would consider him a hero. If he lost his life, it would be a melancholy comfort to them that he lost it in saving some-

61

one else. Thus by his action he might even bring honor to his parents. Not so a Chinese son. A filial Chinese son would remember his parents and would reason that his body belonged to his parents, not to a stranger, and that he therefore had no right to leap into the water at all. If he did so forget himself as to think of the stranger as a human being and put out his hand to save him and thereby lose his own life, he would bring actual shame upon his parents. He should have had more control—he should have thought of them first, of their dependence upon him emotionally, of his duty to them all his life long. He may not risk his life so heedlessly. Now no one will be so foolish as to say that either the Chinese or the American son loves his parents better than does the other. Doubtless they *feel* the same toward their elders. But their ideas of what constitutes honorable behavior in the eyes of their parents is very different indeed. And each is equally idealistic—each equally anxious to conform to what he has been taught is the highest behavior for a son.

In the Orient, therefore, a man will not easily become a soldier. There is no honor in fighting for a cause. There is no such thing as a cause, indeed, in comparison with the responsbility a man has for preserving his life for his family and through his family for society. There are no authentic Oriental patrotic songs. Patriotism as we of the West conceive it is beginning to filter into the Orient, but as an idea as foreign as the airplane. Indeed, the real Oriental attitude is that unless it is to save family honor, the really brave man will resist emotional appeal and will consider his duty to those dependent upon him economically and emotionally. Nor is this lack of courage. The Oriental believes that it takes more courage oftentimes to run away than to fight. It is not an idle saying, "Of the thirty-six ways of escape, the best is to run away." To him anything else is the behavior of a crude and barbarous person. The ungoverned man, the inferior creature, gives way to the impulse of the moment. The civilized mind takes thought and reasons and acts with prudence and with knowledge of the future. He is, in short, really courageous in refusing to be swept by the ignorant and emotional mass.

What one has to remember is that these differences in behavior are not fundamental. That is, they are no more fundamental than the difference in clothes or food or any other external thing. They are prompted by the same feelings that make our young men rush to arms in defense of country, or what they believe to be such defense, and the same feelings which make any American ashamed if he is not physically brave to the point of recklessness. The feelings are exactly the same—the desire to do what is right, that is, what is socially approved—but the acts are diametrically opposite because the ideas of what is right are completely different.

Because ideas are so fundamental, because they are so often what is handed to each generation from the last, because, however we in our time repudiate what has been given us yet we can never wholly escape what we have been given so that there is always a body of fixed ideas in the life of any people, and indeed of any person, and no revolution can change this heritage at root, I want to dwell for a while more fully upon this matter of ideological difference between East and West before I go into the matter of our emotional likeness.

What is the real root of this difference in thinking between East and West? As I see it from my many years of life in the Orient and my few years in my own country, it seems to me that the two people begin thinking from opposite ends. That is, the Chinese reason from the individual to the general, and we reason from the general to the individual. That is, the Chinese principles of living, the Chinese essentials of what constitute justice and righteousness are drawn not from any religion, not from any idealism, but from thousands upon thousands of individual cases. People by and large are so, say the Chinese, the human heart has such and such needs—therefore, law must allow for these needs. Even Confucianism, which is perhaps the most complete code of personal behavior the mind of man has ever devised, was not based on any divine principle of God-given direction, but solely on the prudent taking into account of how, given the surroundings of family and state, emperors and neighbors, rich and poor, a man should conduct himself. But even Confucianism the Chinese have simplified. The human creature on the whole hates laws and rules, say the Chinese, therefore let us have as few laws and rules as possible. It is a Chinese axiom that the best government is the government which rules the least obviously. And further, if a man must be ruled, must be disciplined and punished, it is also obvious that he is most justly dealt with by those who know him best, and with whom he is most directly connected. Therefore let him be controlled, punished, by the members of his own family, and if they fail, by the members of his village. How can laws made at some capital hundreds of miles away and by strangers suit his individual need? He is truly measured not by an abstract law, but by the opinion of his group, and if they approve him, he is not condemned, and if they do not, they will punish him. Only in recent years in China, and this because of Western influence, has there come to be a body of codified, national law. And yet it remains largely upon paper, and the people still live by their own laws of local public opinion. The result of course has been the development in China of an astonishingly adequate system of local self-government, and no people have been more law-abiding, according to their own laws, than have the common people of the village and countryside, literally because the law has been made by the people for the people, and the power of punishment has been local and immediate. Doubtless there has been occasional injustice, where unjust men have had the power for a time, but even there such men have, I believe, come to swifter downfall than elsewhere because the Chinese will not tolerate such injustice long—that is, local injustice. They are, in fact, the most democratic-minded people in the world and bear least patiently oppression from above. They have developed in a high degree the notion of individual right and freedom, as well as individual self-control, and they do not lend themselves easily to the concept of federalized law. The involvement of law to which we are accustomed and by which our huge body of lawyers make their ample livings is of course impossible in China. There government is essentially village government, the village gentry is judge, and neighbors are witnesses and jury. And each man is tried in his own peculiar circumstances. His nature is taken into account, his need, the reason for his crime, the provocation, and he is measured not by any written law, but by whether, in the opinion of his fellows, he was justified, all things taken into consideration, in what he did. If so, then though he committed murder, he may go free. If not, he will die—or at least pay enough money to satisfy the claims of those he has injured, if they prefer his money to his death.

Out of centuries of such individualized justice, of course, a few principles have evolved, but they are principles relating not to any abstract ideas, but solely to a man in relation to his family and neighbors. There are no laws governing his behavior to his nation or to strangers, for to these abstractions he has no relation. A man in his family must behave in certain ways if he is a superior man. So in his public conduct also, if he is a man of superior education. If he is a common fellow, less is expected of him. That is, a man in China is expected to behave in the best way he is able, with his circumstances of birth, breeding, and environment. If he has little, little is demanded, unless he actually injured others, and he is lightly judged. If he has had much, the condemnation is heavier if he falls short. There has been no national constitution, and thereby much time is saved.

Contrast this with our own system of absolute right and wrong. The word *ought* is indispensable in our American thinking. We do not at all obey it more than do other peoples; indeed, since this *ought* is often so far removed from what we are able to do, we perhaps disobey it rather more often than most people do, and hence the number of our lawbreakers. Instead, that is, of thinking about people and discovering what they are able to do, and more important perhaps, what they actually do do and will persist in doing, and basing our laws on this actuality, we make our laws—and I do not mean our federal or state laws only but also our laws of opinion and taste—from some abstract and idealistic and didactic code, devised by dreamers and sometimes fanatics, and then we force individuals to try to shape themselves to these abstractions. The result is, of course, inevitably a good deal of pretense and hypocrisy. It cannot be otherwise, for we are not better or worse than other people, and secretly we like to do about the same sort of thing. If our laws are too rigidly against what we like to do, in time we devise private ways of escape, or we are not able to devise, and we suffer from a feeling of deprivation which is apt to express itself in extreme censorship of others. In any event, the necessity for secrecy, the inability to escape, too often breeds mental and emotional unbalance.

Just why there is this difference between Eastern and

Western thought is difficult to say. Undoubtedly one reason is that Chinese philosophy has on the whole believed that the heart of man is good, while we of the West, influenced largely by our religion, have believed too much and too long that the heart of man is desperately wicked. This sounds rather simple and obvious, but the fact is, I believe, that this simply said thing has had a very far-reaching effect. One feels it in the atmosphere of the two sides of the world. The Chinese, for instance, live far more hardly than we do. The creature comforts of the average man are practically nothing at all, and he is very poor indeed. We here in these United States, in spite of the Depression, have no real idea of poverty in any mass degree. But poverty is the lot of most Chinese. Yet in that poverty they are not degraded, and they walk with a sort of inner freedom and gaiety which I do not feel among us here. Too many of us Americans, though we be comfortable enough, are not really free. That is, we have inside us a little core of gnawing worry, not really economic worry or any other reasonable worry, but a vague unlocalized sense that perhaps we are not doing all we ought about something or other—a sort of unfocused conscience. We live in an inner unease which makes us restless or weary or overexcitable, or gloomy or too nervously pleasure-seeking. It is really an abortive sense of duty, of which we cannot rid ourselves, inherited perhaps from our Puritan forefathers, and fostered by Sunday Schools, Y.W.C.A., boy and girl scouts, and all organizations which urge us to the duty of a kind-deed-a-day sort, so that we lie down uneasily at night upon our pillows unless we have performed. In this day and time we do not greatly fear hell, of course, nor heaven, but we still have with us the atavistic memory of the wicked human heart and that we must struggle, at least a little, to be good or at least to be better than we are, or than we really want to be.

But the Chinese child is not told or taught that he is wicked. Indeed, the average child is not told that he is either wicked or good. He is what he is, and he is accepted as such. If he wants to scream, his elders bear it patiently, because he is a child and because they believe it is bad for anyone to bottle up anger. If the child wants to scream and let out his temper, he may do so, and there is no worry over him because everybody knows he is a child and that when he ceases to be a child he will put away childish things and cease to scream. Surrounded by this calm atmosphere of neither praise nor blame, the child does cease to scream at an amazingly early age. At the same time he has had the experience of screaming all he wants to, and he is not forced to premature self-control, and he grows up without further desire to scream. Nowhere is he taught, at home or in school, that he is not born by nature good. The result is that the Chinese has no sense of personal fault and sin. I do not mean that as a reasonable creature he does not know when he has done wrong about some particular things—that is, has violated the public opinion of his group —but I mean he is not weighed down by any vague, diffuse sense of his inferiority, his personal worthlessness, his inability to achieve his ideals. He is free inside himself. He laughs easily and often. I once asked an intelligent young

Chinese, then a student at Harvard, what he thought of the net result of the Western missionary movement in China. He himself had been in a mission school, and at one time was a Christian. He replied, "We all recognize the truth that missionaries have done us a great social good in hastening modern education, particularly for women, and in introducing Western ideas of science, medicine, and hygiene. But they have also introduced the sense of personal sin, and in this they have clouded the hearts of us all. For myself, I was a happy child, but as a young boy I was sent to a Christian school, and being sensitive, I learned to fear that I was evil without knowing why or being able to help it. My adolescent sex impulses, for instance, which my family considered perfectly natural, I heard were shameful, and I suffered for years with a sense of weakness and inferiority and of being beneath the power of an awful God. Not until I got completely back into my normal home atmosphere was I able to realize that this fear was totally unjustified, that I was neither weak nor depraved, and that I was not sinful by nature. So I was free again."

This illustrates the *ought* in our Western nature, that *ought,* that sense of duty as yet unfulfilled, with which so many struggle. It has, of course, its fruitful aspects. Undoubtedly our inner restlessness and ill adjustment have led the stronger ones among us to greater activity in many fields. In art, in exploration, in science, this restlessness has driven them inexorably onward, forcing them to try to find in activity the satisfaction which they crave, and in the knowledge of achievement gaining, temporarily at least, a sense of peace. The Oriental, not so driven, has found peace without this activity. He is born and reared in tune with his environment, and has enjoyed what he has had without struggling for change or achievement. When he has produced, in art particularly, it has been out of a full heart, at ease with itself and overflowing into expression rather than struggling to achieve expression.

The result is, of course, a gain and a loss. In the East the mass of people are better contented, even in poverty, than they are in the West. There are fewer nervous breakdowns, less mental disturbance, fewer fanatics and cranks of all kinds, more merriment, more simple and hearty enjoyment of life, less pressure of any kind upon the individual. There is also, as we all know, less signal individual achievement in invention and discovery and creation. The perfectly adjusted individual does not feel the need to strive and achieve. It is a truism, surely, that most of our Western achievement has been because certain able individuals were unsatisfied, restless, and unhappy. It will be interesting to discover, some hundreds of years hence when all of us are dead, in the completely socialized nations of that time, when none can profit by anything he does, and when none can starve, when, supposedly, every man is fed, content, and taken care of equally with all others, whether that safety and that content will not produce a sort of vegetation of the creative impulse such as we see in so many Oriental countries, where the family system, with its protective life-long care of the individual, provides what is essential in the socialized state. Certainly it seems that the creative

71

impulse works best in extremes of being—that is, it is impelled by dissatisfaction and unhappiness and ill adjustment to a certain sort of expression, or it is impelled by an overflow of happiness and joy into another sort of expression, both equally valuable. It seems most quiescent when life gives no opportunity for either of these forces to work.

Be that as it may, it is beside my point just now, which is that our Western sense of *ought*—that sense which so directs our ideas in the West, so that we shape our philosophies and our laws upon it, and by it judge all individual action—in China is found, not produced and shaped by abstractions, but gathered from all the multitudinous incidents of life itself, so that philosophy, law, yes, even religion, is completely flexible according to the exigencies of the individual. Or to put it another way, our ideals are taken from an abstract basis; Chinese ideals are taken from life. The result, to recapitulate slightly, is that, since we have tried in the West to force ourselves, both in individual and national life, to an impossible abstract and idealistic standard, we have in the West an extraordinary amount of maladjustment, simply because we will not allow ourselves to view life as it really is. We persist in believing in the ideal world, the world as we wish it were, a heavenly world which never was on land or sea or in the sky. In the East, because there has not been this discrepancy, inevitable between life and the human heart and ideals set in heaven, because ideas on the whole have been those which men could attain in their various stations, there has been greater freedom of the heart and more mental ease and normalcy and certainly more joy—joy, of course, being really totally unrelated to economics, or very nearly so, short of actual starvation. At the same time, the West has gained in achievement because of restlessness engendered by maladjustment, and the East has lost. Longfellow's poem "Excelsior," which so many little American children once had to memorize in public school, would never have been written by a Chinese poet and would be incomprehensible to the Chinese mind. Indeed, it would appear to the average Chinese child as a very silly affair from start to finish, much fuss about an expedition useless from the start, which only a lunatic would have undertaken, when he might have been pleasantly at home, enjoying life with and for others. It is a point of view.

This lack of drive in the East, which, as I have said, I believe comes primarily from a feeling of complete adjustment with the universe, because ideals are not placed in abstraction and the individual is not doomed to a sense of personal failure, has of course another result in the individual, namely, that we do not find in the East as in the West that frequent ambition on the part of an individual to achieve something in his own right; in other words, to become famous as a man. Indeed, fame is, at least in China, a danger and a curse. An individual who rises too high above the average is always viewed with suspicion and alarm as an abnormal creature, and society immediately works to pull him down. We see, of course, the same thing in a less degree in our own society—it may be an instinct natural to the human heart. But certainly it is inevitable in any democracy, where the average or below is the only safety, since anyone above the average threatens the whole democracy. And China has been of course for centuries the only real democracy in the world, with the family functioning as the unit. There is an interesting study waiting to be made by somebody—the history of China as a democracy. Chinese society has been democratic for so long that there we can see democracy gone to seed—such seed as we ourselves will be producing if we persist in our democratic ways for a few centuries. Unless we go socialistic or fascistic we shall do exactly what China has done—we may not develop the family as our individual unit, but we will develop some other unit as our protection of the individual in a democratic society, where each one of us must fear the power of the other, and where the person, as one, cannot stand alone and survive. And one seed, at least, in the Chinese democracy is that the ambition of the individual is curbed and controlled, and achievement beyond the extraordinary is viewed with dislike, jealousy, and alarm by other individual units.

So much, all too generally, for what seems to be the fundamental difference in what we think, East and West.

But about these differing ideas and ideals we feel the same way. Alike we admire the man who achieves the ideal, though what constitutes the ideal man, East and West, is not the same. In the West, for instance, the man, because he is a man, struggles against showing emotion, against tears, particularly against showing fear. In the East the man weeps unaffectedly and unfeignedly, and to feel fear

74

and show it is no shame—rather, indeed, a sign that he is of a sensitive and highly intelligent type, since only coarse and brutal persons are too insensitive to feel fear. I have had many people here in the West express surprise because the young Chinese hero in one of my books wept occasionally in distress. To them it seemed proof of weakness. But in China tears are tears, whether shed by man or woman, and for a man not to weep at the death of a near relative or friend or in other distress would be absurd and inhumanly hard conduct. In Chinese novels the weeping of the great hero is described at length, his eyes running tears in streams, his nostrils dripping a foot long, his saliva unchecked, his sobs loud and regular, runs the usual stereotyped phraseology. But what we have to realize is that the Chinese admire courage as much as we do and they feel the same way about it. Only in China a brave man may weep if he suffers, and his tears do not mean he is not brave.

This difference in the way we express similar emotion has of course led to much misunderstanding. Take, for example, the very common belief in the West that the Chinese is inscrutable, sly, secret. Nothing could be farther from the truth concerning either Chinese or Japanese or, for that matter, any Oriental whom I know. The Chinese is an extraordinarily emotional creature who, when you are on any terms of friendship with him at all, shows his emotion with almost embarrassing candor. He is the least repressed of persons, and of a mercurial and vivid temperament. His feelings are strong but changeful. He is on the whole incapable of sustained unchanged emotion. He responds with almost touching instancy to friendliness and affection and trust. Once he has made a friend he is extraordinarily loyal. But the rather childlike quality of his lack of repression makes him also a vengeful enemy, quick to take offense, instant to seek retribution. But if an apology is given sincerely, he is as quick to forgive and to forget injury.

But I find in the United States, particularly, almost complete misunderstanding of the emotional nature of the Chinese. I think this is because of the very false impression we have gained from motion pictures and books written by casual persons, and by writers in search of villains whom they dare not take from the life near them. And partly, of course, we get our idea from the Chinese about us, who, like all foreigners in a strange land, draw together and present to strangers a mute and defensive inscrutability. White colonies living in Chinese communities present the same look to the Chinese. They are aliens, living on sufferance, in an alien civilization, dressing in different garments, eating different foods, behaving in different customs, maintaining themselves with difficulty and a great deal of determination. The result is that the very face of the alien, whether he is Chinese in America, or Amercan in China, takes on a closed, inscrutable look. How often have I heard a Chinese on the street, watching a foreigner, turn and say to his neighbor, "One can tell nothing from the faces of these foreigners. Good or evil, it is all locked behind their strange language and their pale looks." Which translated into American is, "Gee, these foreigners give me the willies!"

But this very thing is an illustration of my point—that we feel the same, East and West—we even feel the same about each other!

The truth is that of all people, Oriental and Occidental, Americans and Chinese, should best understand each other, because temperamentally we are extraordinarily alike. I find, for instance, my life in the United States not strange at all—strange in certain external ways, perhaps, in mechanical devices which seem to me too often stronger and wiser than I am, but not basically strange. This is because the people here feel and are the same kind of people that I lived among in China. The same changefulness, the same tendency to love today and hate tomorrow, the same love of pleasure and good food and luxury, the same tendency toward large, lavish expenditure, the same generosity combined with an extraordinary and shrewd selfishness, the same love of tall stories and extravagant statement, the same disregard for accurate truth, the same huge love of a joke, the same swift emotional life, only here made secret by the American *ought,* and in China channeled into recognized allowances for human nature. Japan is another story. The real reason why we do not like Japan as well as China is because the Japanese are emotionally different from ourselves. They are much more like the English than they are like the Americans, and you will find in England more secret sympathy with Japan than you will with China.

They feel the same—they have the same admiration for control and physical bravery and self-denial and national pride and rectitude and detail.

I believe of course that these emotional likenesses and differences are due not to race, for race is extraordinarily meaningless in explaining fundamental differences. Much more probably they are due simply to geography. That is, peoples living, as do the Chinese and ourselves, in broad, rich, abundant lands—in continents, really—upon landscapes varying from seacoast and northern cold to high mountains and tropical plains, come to be alike. The variety of our climate and our foods produces variety in our nature; the many-sidedness of nature about us forces us to develop many-sidedness in ourselves. We learn to adapt to all sorts of life, and we shape life in many ways. The very expanse and size of our lands influence us, and the richness of our produce encourages in us a sense of confidence and power and plenty. The lands of the United States and of China are extraordinarily alike—the northern plains in China and our western plains, the deserts of north and west, the rich central plains of both countries, the long seacoast, the vast, long rivers, the bleakness of the north and the tropics of the south, the self-sufficiency of both countries, the similarity of the food produced with, I think, the higher honor given to the Chinese cooks—here are great similarities, inevitably producing, or so I think, similarities in temperament. The element in us which is unlike, namely our ideas, exists simply because our forefathers brought over with them from small struggling compressed

European countries certain hard religious ideas and the fearfulness of pioneer life enhanced the force of these ideas. But now as our life circumstances more nearly approach those of the older people, the Chinese, as our population is increasing, economic life is necessarily becoming more like that of the Chinese, and when our geography is like that of the Chinese, and our economy increasing like theirs, the chances are that our ideas will become increasingly like theirs. Indeed, this is already true. We are in the transition stage between a new and an old people. The Puritan rigor of our ideals is giving way, not necessarily to lower ideals, but to more human ones, at least. These transition generations are distressed and caught in the change, and have not the sureness of old or new, but they are transition. When we have passed into the period in which the Chinese have been for many centuries, I think we shall find our ideas, even, becoming increasingly like theirs—that is, we shall modify, even as we are now beginning to do, our ideas of abstract right and wrong, to suit what the human heart is able to perform.

In the same way, it is interesting to see the likeness between England and Japan carried out in many temperamental ways, and again I believe it is because geographically they are so much alike—island peoples compelled by chance to small space, at the mercy of the sea, and peoples made vigorous by the very exigencies and hardships of their life, so that extreme loyalty to a common code, great physical courage, patriotism, and the dream of empire, or in other words, the chance to expand, realized long since by

England and still the hope of Japan—these are integral parts of English and Japanese nature alike. China, like the United States, has not been an imperialistic nation because neither of us has been compelled to be, and we have not therefore developed the strength and the weakness of the imperialistic temperament. But we would have developed them if we had been caught and held in small island space, our food limited to a few acres and what we could catch from the sea.

In brief, then, our emotions are not so much the result of our ideas or our religion as of the food we eat and the land and the climate in which we live, and because China and the United States are so much alike in these respects, we are very much alike in the way we feel.

This emotional likeness manifests itself in many ways. I might give you a real catalogue of all these ways, for there they are, large and small. But I shall again confine myself to a few of the larger and more fundamental ones. The chiefest, I think, is the one I have already mentioned, the changefulness of our emotions. In China, as in the United States, no creature will be more despised tomorrow than the hero of today. The cycle of popularity through which every popular favorite in the United States must pass, from President to baseball player, is a cycle of Cathay also. The experience which Roosevelt is now having is exactly the same that Chiang Kai-shek is having, only he has stayed in some sort of office long enough to have lived through several cycles. Butterfly Wu, for several years the screen favorite in Shanghai, has shared the fate of Greta Garbo here. It is not the fault of the individual—it is simply the quality of the temper of the peoples, who must continually see and hear something new, and to whom nothing can remain dear for long. Both Chinese and American, therefore, must be characterized as peoples by temperament shallow. Clever they both are, highly intelligent, technically quick to learn any new thing. But from them nothing profound may be expected, nothing that takes long, tenacious effort. Chinese, as much as Americans, or almost as much, want quick and showy results. The sciences, I believe, when they develop again into the stage of invention in China, will take the same trend they have taken in our country, namely, that of mechanical and applied science, rather than of pure science and fundamental philosophical discovery.

Another emotional likeness between the two peoples is that of pride and self-sufficiency. I suppose this feeling of self-sufficiency is inevitable in any people who have large territory and varied agriculture—the feeling of enough land for food, of space enough of one's own, must always breed pride and contempt for the foreigner. Certainly there is less international interest and comprehension in these two countries than in any others of which I know, and less consideration is given to the foreigner within their borders than is given in other civilized countries. The attitude of the average Chinese toward foreign peoples and foreign problems is exactly that of the average American. I have been actually startled sometimes to hear the precise words uttered by an American that I have heard a Chinese utter. It was like hearing a phonograph record. And upon the streets and in our life the foreigner is given the same treatment that he receives in China—the treatment of a careless person intent upon his own affairs and not concerned with those of other peoples. I do not call it the superiority complex so much as the simple attitude of the careless person, the person made careless and insensitive by plenty of life of his own.

There is a good deal of cruelty, as a matter of fact, in both peoples, by temperament, a sort of childish cruelty, cruelty to inferiors when they are helpless, mingled at the same time with a great deal of sudden good-humored kindness when it does not interfere with selfish interests. For the Chinese, like the Americans, are primarily governed by commercial instincts, and as yet business is always Big, and even their kindness and friendliness is often tempered by shrewdness.

So they are alike in many ways. They are full of life and gusto, physically vigorous, and mentally alert, but they are not religious or poetic except in isolated individual cases. They have not the poetic strain of the Irish, or even of the English, not the deep religious tinge of the Scotch or the Japanese, not the mysticism of the Hindu. Indeed, religiously, except for the content of their ideas, the religious emotions of the American and the Chinese are remarkably alike—that is, they do not really exist. Such religious life as they have is expressed in rather materialistic forms, and in group and social ways rather than in true religious experience, which is, I believe, always individual.

Americans and Chinese—they both love to eat, to play, to be amused. How the Americans and the Chinese love to be amused, and how they will forgive anyone anything if only he amuses them! How long Jimmy Walker, even while he was Mayor of New York, was tolerated and even adored because he amused people, and how long warlords in China are tolerated and even adored if they are amusing! Even a foreigner has saved his life by being able to turn a joke at the right second, when his life hung in the balance. Charlie Chaplin is the idol of the Shanghai screen.

And how sentimental they are—these Chinese and Americans—how they will sob over home and mother, and how they will weep in their theaters and how indignant they will become for a moment because of some crime and how if they are angry enough for a moment they will take a man out and hang him or behead him, and then in an instant forget all about it and do nothing at all until they are angry again! And how they adore pretty, silly, little women! Chinese men, too, sit and moon over the femininity of Janet Gaynor, China's American sweetheart.

And so it all goes. There is, I fear, nothing new under the sun, as the Ecclesiastic said a good many centuries ago —forgetting that even then the saying was not new. The same kind of land, feeding the same kinds of foods, under the same sun and winds, the shores washed by the same seas, will produce the same kind of hearts and minds, however the skins may differ. The skin, the color of the hair and eyes—these are, after all, only a kind of dress given us by our chance parents, and not more important than dress ever is. Inside we have the same heart and lungs, the same organs by means of which we live and feel and are.

6

The Chinese Attitude Toward Graft

ONE OF THE SUBJECTS the foreigner in China loves most to expatiate upon is graft. Sooner or later the visitor there must hear long complacent explanations of the prevalence of graft in every part of Chinese life, and he learns that though the crusader and missionaries may fight their hearts out trying to change it, the wise man learns to accept it and look upon graft as a part of Chinese life—the habit of centuries.

Whether it is true that graft permeates all Chinese life I do not know. It is true that in private as well as in public life certain forms of graft are accepted. The servants in my Chinese household, for instance, have a regular part of their income from "squeeze." This is clearly understood and the proceeds are fairly divided among them. The cook gets five percent of all grocery bills, and he charges me from

Article in Harper's, *January, 1935. Copyright renewed, 1963, by Pearl S. Buck.*

five to ten percent extra on all purchases he makes for me in the market. The house boys get five percent on all laundry bills, on shoes made for the family, on all tailor bills, on all purchases made at shops or from dealers at the door. The gardener, who also in winter takes care of the furnace, gets five percent of all coal bills and garden necessities, and on taxis or vehicles I hire. Every expenditure made for the household is taxed not less than five percent, not more than ten percent, by the servants. This form of graft is perfectly open and known, of course, and the wise mistress ignores it.

In shops the clerks may also get certain percentages on sales, or certain reductions on goods. The land purchaser expects his commission, naturally, and beyond this a good feast if a bargain is made. In official life graft takes three chief forms: illegal taxes, privately imposed by officials over and beyond official taxes, as well as actual falsification of amounts of official taxes collected so that a certain proportion is retained by the official; nepotism and "friend pidgin"; and third, the graft which results from the attitude common to many officials anywhere, that laws are made for the common people only and rulers are above them.

The evils of unjust and illegal taxation are perhaps the most real which the Chinese people have to endure. The rapid change in officialdom of the last few years, the constant pressing of civil war which gives generals a permanent excuse for extortion on the grounds of defending the peace, the lack of a really strong central authority, have all made it possible for taxes to be collected in many regions as long as ten years in advance, and in a few regions even fifty years in advance. Besides this, officials have superimposed all sorts of special famine relief taxes or "patriotic" taxes or opium preventive taxes and many others, and since there is no required accounting for such accumulations, it is beyond doubt that most of it goes into the pockets of collectors and officials.

Nepotism, of course, must exist on a large scale where the family is still the ruling unit, as it is in China. So long as a family is responsible for the support of any and all indigent and disabled members, so long must it be expected that a man will fill any posts at his disposal with jobless nephews and brothers in order to ease his own burden. Moreover, there is a certain reasonableness in this, for in China the family still performs the duties which in many Western countries are performed by the state. There are no state institutions for the poor, the aged, the helpless, or the defective. Each family must care for its own. The result is much the same as in other countries, but the funds are collected differently. The public pays in either case, in the West by open taxation, in the East by more devious means.

"Friend pidgin" is only an enlarged nepotism. A man helps his friends in the time of his prosperity as an investment against a possible or probable day of adversity. When such a day comes, he may go boldly and without shame to this friend and that and ask for aid, since once he aided them. It is a guarantee of security in a society full of insecurity, where, since there are no public laws of government to stand upon, each man, commoner or governor, must forge as strongly as he can the personal laws of family and friendship.

How peculiar it is to the Chinese official or great man to feel himself above the laws of the land I do not know. I have not yet seen enough of the mighty in other countries to find out whether this trait is chiefly Oriental or not, although my observation in other lines leads me to feel there is no such thing as a purely Oriental quality of human nature. Any one thing may be more or less in the Orient, and less or more in the Occident. But in China, at any rate, one of the real obstacles in modern times has been the tendency of officials high and low, and all rich men and men of influence and place, to think that laws are made only for the poor and common folk, who do not know how to behave. Here the graft may not be in actual cash, but in some form of special privilege.

But there is no way of making comparisons about graft in East and West. One of the difficulties which confronts the expatriate of any country is the spiritual dilemma in which his soul must live forever unsure. Briefly it may be stated thus: is or is not my own country better as regards graft than this one in which I live as a foreigner?

To this there is no answer, of course, although the expatriate does not realize it for many years, and perhaps never. He continues to reply, first in one way and then another, depending upon the experience of the day. A wily servant or a tricky merchant in China will set the white man growling with homesickness for his own honest countrymen. A day in New York or Chicago sends his heart flying across the Pacific again, hurt and seeking refuge in the Chinese, who at least do not pretend to Puritan heights of perfection.

The confirmed expatriate however, at least in China, tends to idealize his own people the longer he stays away from his country. He usually belongs to a small and ruling group of white men and his society becomes ingrowing and self-congratulatory. He compares himself and his fellows not with their equals or superiors in Chinese circles, but with that person, the servant or the coolie or the compradore, who is all too frequently, and unfortunately, the only one with whom he comes into intimate contact. Because his servant takes a squeeze of five dollars a month, he believes General Wang takes a squeeze of a million dollars a month. Because a wretched ricksha puller trades off a false coin for change, he believes the president of a Chinese bank capable of peculation on a large scale, as indeed he doubtless sometimes is, in common with his fellow bankers in other lands.

But the expatriate forgets this. He asserts loudly that in a white man's country "such things couldn't happen." Officials are more honest—"they *have* to be," he says, "or the people wouldn't stand for them." He views with the utmost disgust the placid Chinese who accepts without disturbance graft in high places and low, although be sure he is not ignorant of it.

And the expatriate has something to be said for him. To a certain degree, in a certain way, he is right. There is a difference between Americans and Chinese. Americans do not apparently view so nonchalantly as the Chinese this matter of graft. There seems to be knowledge everywhere of graft in our political and economic systems, but the American, when he discovers proof of it, is highly irritated by it, and he demands punishment if possible of a fairly severe sort.

The reason for this hatred of graft on the part of the average American is as yet fairly obscure to me. It cannot be simply moral for too often he succumbs to similar temptation when opportunity comes. The number of Americans who are willing and even eager to get something for nothing seems not noticeably fewer than similar Chinese. Public robbery of some kind or other apparently permeates our American life if one is to believe what one reads. A headwaitress in a certain well-known chain restaurant in a large city told me the other day that they had to exercise constant vigilance because there was scarcely a mealtime when there were not persons who tried to pass the cashier's desk without paying for what they had eaten. I inquired if these were poor people, to which she replied, "We don't get real poor people coming in here. No, they just want to get away with something."

I have been told by civil servants that persons who receive their salaries out of public funds tend, unless they struggle against it, to become lazy and lax, and look upon such funds not as a trust to be wisely expended, but as an inexhaustible supply—an attitude common to public servants in any country. My own observations in a small way

89

show me nothing new in America as compared with China. How many times have I cautiously slowed my car at a sign on the highway which proclaims MEN WORKING, and how seldom have I discovered them working here in America even as they do not in China! And graft on a princely scale is of course to be discovered on the front pages of many American newspapers.

But here I halt. There is a difference in the American and Chinese attitude toward graft. Graft is not a matter for headlines in Chinese papers. It is not of sufficient interest. It is not news. In America surely it cannot be news either, yet the discovery of it is always a public excitement. It is quite true that the situation regarding graft itself is not so much fundamentally different in the two countries as that the two peoples have two different attitudes toward graft.

Now I do not believe that this difference in attitude toward a fairly well known fact of life anywhere springs from a real inequality in morals. The Chinese and the American may moralize about different things. The American may be more or less conscientious on the subject of lying and the Chinese on the matter of obeying his parents so long as they live. But they are equally capable of moral principles, of developed conscience and consistent action. Moral nature cannot therefore explain this difference in attitude upon graft, an evil common to both peoples.

The main difference is not basically moral at all. It has nothing to do with right and wrong. It is simply the difference between anger and good humor in a man when he discovers his pocket has been picked in a crowd. I venture to say there would be undoubtedly a larger number of Chinese who, the first shock over, would grin and accept the loss than there would be similar Americans. At least I can see the American protesting more vigorously against his fate in one way or another. This is partly because to balance his native delight in being able to "put something over," the American has an extreme distaste for having something "put over" on him. In public graft that "something" is funds to which the average man has been forced to contribute, and when graft is discovered he feels robbed as an individual and is angry. This is of course a very healthy natural anger and may have its effect in bringing lower, at least, the proud and mighty grafter and intimidating the lesser ones.

But the Chinese would say calmly, "Why should I expend my precious life force in anger against an evil I cannot hope ever in my lifetime to overcome by any amount of anger? The evil is universal, it must remain universal, *so long as things are as they are.* It only behooves me to be more watchful, more distrustful, to avoid, in so far as I am able, being at the mercy of anyone. If I am helpless, as I must be before a public official, let me bide my time until his hour is come, and then I will join in his downfall. For heaven does not allow the evil to live forever. When Heaven strikes I will strike." And he buttons his pocket more securely for the future.

Nor does his philosophy prevent his making use of any of his own opportunities, if he is so minded, although I do not believe that there are more sticky palms in China than elsewhere in the world—certainly not if they are friendly palms. Nowhere can there be a higher standard of friendship, where literally a friend is closer than a brother. A friend who makes profit from a friend is held despicable. But it is only human to profit by the stranger and by those whom one dislikes. It is not wrong for a shopkeeper to double the price of an article on his counter when a foreigner asks for it. He has no relation to the foreigner and there is no reason why he should not profit by his passing. But let some circumstance make a friendliness between the two and the price will fall to its proper scale. There is something above profit even to a shopkeeper. There is *li,* there is right conduct.

This ruling reasonable principle of *li* (pronounced "lee") governs even graft in China. It makes the Chinese accept philosophically the picking of his pocket, for the thief was in his way exercising his right to a living. It makes him accept with equanimity the squeeze of his cook, for so cooks have always done, and the wage is fixed with this in the minds of both. He accepts also with equal equanimity the larger squeeze of the magistrate who rules over him, for magistrates must live as well as cooks, and he has his rights, too.

There is only one time when philosophy fails, and it is when cook or magistrate takes more than he should—when, in other words, he violates *li,* or reason, and behaves outrageously. Then, be he cook or magistrate, his end is come. I have seen a mob of angry farmers, who were patient and without complaint under years of illegal taxation, suddenly rise with grim ferocity and sack a magistrate's court and drive him out or even kill him, not because he grafted, but because he grafted too much and beyond what was expected of him. At that hour men could rise up in protest, for the right was with them and it was heaven's will.

The whole scheme of life then in China is based on acceptance of a certain amount of inevitable graft. Official salaries, as well as servant's wage, take it into consideration. Where no monies pass and there is no possibility of graft, the wage rises accordingly. College professors are paid relatively well, as are all teachers and clerks who handle no funds. In a way, therefore, graft does less injury to the public in China than it does in America, where the scheme ignores or denies the possibility of graft, where the wage scale is immeasurably higher, and where graft is so much extra, both to him who gains and to him who loses by it.

But if morals have little or nothing to do with the different attitude toward graft between the two countries, there is another basic cause for the difference. This is that the Chinese are more rational than Americans. They are rational above all people on earth. They do not blindly accept things as they are. They are not truly fatalistic in the passive and nonintelligent sense of the word. But they do accept things as they are until they can be changed in one way or another. However they may plan to deceive the stranger, among themselves they acknowledge completely and without pretense their every situation. No fair words put forth by a governor or a general ever deceive any Chinese. Behind the noble, flowery phrases he casts up quickly the cost of what is wanted. If it is within reason or if the circumstances are beyond his control he pays what he cannot escape. If the cost is too great, there are ways.

For the Chinese is wise in life. He does not demand of his officials an impossible purity. He knows his own frail human heart, how easily he himself is tempted and how naturally he fails, and shrewdly he surmises that if his own heart is thus frail, every other is at least as likely to be so. Nor does this mean that the Chinese is bitter or even cynical —quite the reverse, since there is no one so really bitter or so entirely cynical as the disappointed idealist who discovers human nature. The workaday Chinese is without romantic idealism and he is not disappointed. He remains good-humored and if he makes allowances for himself, so does he for everyone else. In a country where every office is unstable, where today's government may tomorrow be overthrown, where a general of the morning may be decapitated by night or taking refuge in a foreign tour, he knows graft is to be expected. The future must be provided for; the hour of downfall must be anticipated. An official has always a large family, an entourage, who are dependent upon him and whose future rice must be prepared. In any insecure society where the individual must fight his lone way, at the mercy of others stronger than he, graft is absolutely inevitable. No public wage is large enough to provide against fear. A man, faced continually with the possibility of change and downfall, and with many dependent upon him, must be superhuman to resist taking all he can. And the Chinese recognize the fact that circumstances determine morals. Indeed, it may even be moral for a man to squeeze, since his first duty is to his family and he must provide for them at any cost. It is his highest responsibility, for according to Chinese code, a man must care for his parents first, and then his own children and wife and brothers and sisters. It is a primary crime if these are destitute.

This does not mean that the Chinese are not making fairly consistent efforts particularly toward steadying their governmental offices sufficiently to provide the security necessary to diminish graft. They are trying to do so, and certainly the trend is toward building up a public opinion which demands a more honest officialdom. But they do not make impossible demands even upon their highest officials until it is fair to do it. The foundation of security must be built before a sound superstructure of official honesty can be built.

The Chinese mind is too essentially rational to set up a standard for character which the conditions of the times make impossible of fulfillment. And they can wait. They know what is right and advisable. Like all other peoples, they prefer honest officials, and the honest man, whether worker or ruler, is worthy of honor. But the ideal is not tarnished because it is not now possible to fulfill it, nor is a man dishonorable because it is not convenient or expedient or possible for him in his present circumstances to achieve the ideal which he very well knows and would like to achieve if he could.

I am here reminded of an incident in my own household where my gardener took a higher graft on our coal bill than he should. Embarrassed by the fact that his morality was obviously to my benefit, I diffidently approached him from another plane. I suggested that he might be happier in himself if he were a really honest man. He was cleaning out ashes at the time, and he turned an earnest, smutty face toward me and answered stoutly, "My mistress, of course I would like to be an honest man. Of course I should be better satisfied with myself. But how can I? If I were to turn truly honest, in a year I and my family would be dead of starvation. If the world could be exactly divided into one-half honest people and one-half dishonest, I would gladly take a chance and join the honest ones. But when all the world is dishonest, how can I so utterly throw aside my duty to my family?"

Against such logic I was silent, for indeed I had no answer.

Honesty must be made possible before it can be made essential. This is, of course, what the American cannot realize. The whole philosophies of the two peoples start from opposite poles. The Chinese starts with knowledge of life as it is and makes his deductions of what it ought to be and expects no sudden miracles, knowing well how easily compelled is the human heart. The American, born of his Puritan forefathers and nourished by an idealistic religion which does not connect itself with the actual life of the nation, begins his philosophy in dreams and builds his laws on what ought to be rather than what can be.

For essentially there is as much insecurity in American life as in Chinese. Even in so-called normal times, for we can set off the effects of our Depression against the usual flood-famine-war combinations in China, the insecurity in American political life at least is enormous. Every major official, for instance, knows that he holds his place secure only for four years. He must make it worthwhile in one way or another to leave his usual business and go into government. It is inevitable that many such persons must feel temptation, at least, very heavy upon them.

Nor have we, as did the Chinese, particularly in the past, any safeguard of natural selection. That is, democracy of the American variety provides no means of choosing the more intelligent and benevolent minds to govern others. The examination system of old China, the high educational standard of new China, provide a fairly sure selection of at least the best of the nation, and therefore those who will have more conscience on the taking of graft than would the average man. In America we have not even so selective a system as in the English democratic government, where there is a certain *noblesse oblige* among able minds to take an active part in government. It is inevitable, therefore, that where conditions are so ideally prepared for graft as they are in America, graft must exist on a large scale, whether the idealist will face it or not. The Chinese realist— naturalist, if you like—would acknowledge it and set about removing root causes, if he could, rather than being content to punish notorious individual cases and ignore the whole basic condition. Or if he could do nothing basic, he would, as he has done in the past and is doing now, set certain recognized limits to the evil, choosing to do this rather than to live in a world of fantasy and of seeming rather than actuality. For the American is an incurable romantic, who will turn away from anything "depressing," whether it be in life or in literature. He says, "I see enough evil—I want to think about something pleasant." So he escapes into a false heaven. The Chinese says, "Is this life? Let me know it, since it is all I can know, evil and good." And he finds content and peace in knowing and in adjusting his inner life to his knowledge. He can no longer be hurt, since he knows everything.

For he recognizes, this wise Chinese, wise when he is born, whose elders teach him an old wisdom of how to live happily in a hard world, that the moral nature of man is not a fixed thing, nor can religion or philosophy fix it. Honesty, like all the other virtues, is entirely relative and relative fundamentally to but one condition and that is economic. When a people is rich and prosperous, doors need not be locked and goods may be left unheeded. But in times of distress and need, whether individual or not, standards change. When the distress becomes national, there is a widespread change of habits of honesty.

There are of course perfectly obvious examples of this in our own times. Seven years ago I chanced to spend a few months in an American university town. No one thought of locking up anything. I went away for days at a time leaving my house unlocked. It was an amazement to me, accustomed as I had been to a very different state of affairs in China. As a Chinese friend of mine, who happened to be in the same American town, put it, "I have been here three years, and although no one locks his house, I have not heard man or woman complain of being robbed." I returned to China overwhelmed with respect for my own countrymen.

But last year I returned to the same town and immediately felt more at home. I was told I must keep my door locked even though I left the house for a half hour. There were so many thieves about. What had happened? Simply that economic conditions in America were approaching those which China has had to struggle under for decades, and human nature responded in America as it had in China. A man is not above his fellows, and never has it been more clearly proven than in the changing moral standards in many American communities with the continued Depression. America is much more like China today than she was seven years ago. If the Depression should continue indefinitely, in fifty years, perhaps less, there would be little or no difference in our living conditions and inevitably, therefore, in our standards of honesty.

The Chinese, then, in his attitude toward graft does not demand what is above human ability to perform. In hard times, in insecure tenure, in economic depression, he knows what must result. A national life of forty centuries, with innumerable wars and vast depressions, has taught him wisdom, and we of America are just beginning that road which the Chinese has traveled for so long. I suppose somewhere upon the way we, too, will learn to view without romanticism life as it really is, and will find it humorous and worth living, grafters and all.

7

China Wins

To WRITE ABOUT the China of today and the China of even a year ago is to write about two very different countries. A year ago an article about China, or even talk about China, might have been filled with all sorts of pleasant things, amusing but of no great importance—what they ate, what they wore, how they amused themselves and how their everyday life went. Today everything is different. I cannot believe there is a corner of China which is untouched and unchanged by this war with Japan. This China is a China in desperate struggle, gathering herself together as she never has, for her existence, a China serious-minded as she has never been before to face her crisis. And Japan, too, is grim and determined, and is bending every energy of her highly organized, closely controlled society to the one end of victory. Upon the outcome of this war between two great Oriental nations the life of nearly a third of the world's

Written in 1938.

100

people depends. And more than that, for all of us are involved in some degree—no one knows to what degree.

What has led to this crisis? How did China come to this pass? Why are the Japanese fighting the Chinese at all? Any Chinese will tell you that China has always been a peaceful, peace-loving nation, and that she has never fought aggressive wars or been interested in aggression. Any Japanese will tell you, astoundingly, that this is a war of goodwill—that is, Japan really wants peace, peaceful trade, and friendly cooperation with China, and that China has made this impossible by her behavior toward Japan. As in any fight, both sides are wrong and both sides are right. Let us think of China's side of it first.

It is true that China has never been an aggressive nation. She has never needed to be. Early in her history her dominant race settled into a huge territory, half again as large as the United States, and conquered that country and pushed back or absorbed the wild tribes lying within it. China is a magnificent country physically. Its climate ranges from the cold northern temperatures of Peiping to the tropic heat of Canton, from the long seacoast of the Pacific, filled with fine harbors and prosperous ports, to the gorgeous mountains of Tibet. Between those extremes lie the deserts of the northwest, the rich plains and fields of central China, and the fertile lands of the south.

It is a beautiful country, with the finest scenery in the world. No wonder Chinese painters so loved landscapes. They had only to look from their windows to see the most lovely pictures: strange tall mountains of rock, and swift, narrow waterfalls, lakes, rivers, misted bamboo-covered hills, and broad streams. I used to think, since I grew up in the rich midlands of China, that the old painters, who lived for the most part in the north, had made up those fantastic mountains from the stuff of their dreams, cliff rising upon cliff, gray in the sunlight, opal in the sunrise and evening. But later when I went to north China and saw for myself those wind-bitten mountains—skeletons, whose flanks for centuries have been beaten upon by bitter winds from the Gobi Desert, until every shred of earth and vegetation has been swept away—I saw they were not dreams but a reality strange and beautiful. And when I went south, into Fukien, I saw other landscapes, mountains green and feathered with palm and bamboo, and orange groves of a size and perfection of planting and arrangement which might teach even the Californians something.

And everywhere were people, people, the tall, strong, handsome people of the north, who look like the American Indians must have looked before their degeneration; the gay, well-fed, solid-looking people of the prosperous midlands of the Yangtze valley; and the small, dark energetic Chinese of the south, who are to be seen most frequently here in America, plain of face because their blood is mixed with the wild blood of the aboriginals who had the land before the Chinese came into it.

Did the Chinese take the land from other people? I must say they did, in those far-off early days on the edge of history. But they took it more often by absorption, by mingling of blood, than by war. They overcame peoples by marrying them and prevailing over them peacefully. China is the only country, for instance, I believe, which has ever absorbed the Jewish race on a large scale. A great many Jews went to China, first and last, and there was even a considerable settlement of Jews about the city of Kaifeng in the province of Honan. There was a synagogue and there was a flourishing Jewish community. It is all gone except a few heaped stones of the synagogue, but through the Chinese of that region, and spreading into all the nation, as famine drove people southward and mixed them together, there runs an occasional Jewish look, an aquiline profile, a turn of the eyelid that is not Chinese but Jewish, curly hair instead of straight, even a custom or a rite that is performed in a Jewish fashion, though mixed with Buddhism. If you ask such a man his name, he will give you a Chinese name, and if you ask him why at a certain time of the year he does a certain thing, he will say he does not know, except that his father and grandfather did. Usually he has a dim memory about the name of Moses, and he will perhaps tell you that once his ancestors came from over the mountains. But he is Chinese, and as far back as he has ever heard, his family have been Chinese.

The Chinese, therefore, have been peacefully aggressive in the lands which they took as their own. I doubt they planned any active peaceful aggression, even. Probably communities simply spread and settled farther and farther inland. And it is true that they never carried a war beyond their final boundaries. Certain adjacent countries, as China grew strong and rich, began to be afraid of her, and to placate her they sent her emperors presents which gradually took the form of tribute, and these nations came to be looked upon as vassal nations.

Within herself, however, China has never been a peaceful nation. The Chinese are not warlike so much as quarrelsome. They are in the position of a large and well-to-do family, with enough people to be self-sufficient, and just keeping peace among themselves satisfies all their fighting instincts. A large family in any community does comparatively little quarreling, perhaps because there is so much to do at home. And in China, with the great variety of people and the variety, indeed, of everything, there has always been civil war of one sort or another. This was partly because means of communication have developed very slowly. Communities have kept to themselves and become isolated. The strong family system aided this isolation, for families stayed together and there was not much wandering. It was easy, therefore, as these communities grew in population, for quarrels to begin and to develop into civil wars. In all my years in China I never knew the country to be at peace within its own borders except for a few years after 1900. Then the revolution of 1911 broke out, and from then on there was never any more peace.

Who was fighting whom? One warlord was fighting another—that is the background of Chinese civil war and it has been until today; and the foreground was the new element of Chinese life, the modern element, born and fostered by Western education, revolting against the old traditional government, and finally successfully overthrowing it, and after another revolution, establishing the government which we call today the National Government of China, whose capital was at Nanking, but has now been driven farther west by the Japanese advance. They too had to fight one warlord after another, however, and these warlords have never been really vanquished, merely driven back. Some of them have been taken into the national armies as generals—indeed the leading generals in the National Army of China today are warlords of yesterday, and I see that while they are allied with the National Army under Chiang Kai-shek, they are not doing much real fighting yet. I doubt they ever do much fighting against Japan—not enough to risk losing their individual armies. After all, they are individualists, with their own armies, and if Japan wins, they want to be in the position to withdraw themselves and their armies into the mountains again, and if Japan loses, they are not at all sure what sort of nation China will be, and they want to be able to get out of it safely. A warlord without his army is in the position of a king with no crown, or a captain with no ship. His army is at once his power and his livelihood.

Of course any patriotic Chinese will tell you that China has no warlords nowadays. I sit back and hear them say this sort of thing and simply smile, knowing the demands of patriotism. China has always had warlords and has them now, and perhaps will have them forever—I don't know. It is a pity to be ashamed of them, for they are really extra-ordinary men—great men, for whom society has found no place, and who therefore go outside of society and gather about them their supporters and friends. It is inevitable in any nation where the central government has always been weak that such characters arise. We have such men in our own country, but in a lesser way, because our government is relatively stronger than that of China.

But these warlords have had an enormous place in Chinese history. Every imperial dynasty was established by a warlord. The Chinese have always been a democratic people, as they are today. Their classes are fluid, as ours are. The log cabin tradition is strong among them, though they call it the grass hut instead of the log cabin. But it is exactly the same thing. Anyone with sufficient ability could and did rise as high as he liked. And the story of empire in China is simply the story of some two dozen warlords, each of them a common fellow rising up from priesthood or peasantry, strong, discontented men who were angered by some condition and left society, taking with them other malcontents, and set up little independent realms. When the dynasty grew weak, and emperors grew lazy and effete, the warlords would begin to fight among themselves, and after a series of civil wars (lasting once for four hundred years) there would remain the strongest warlord and he would ascend the throne and found a new dynasty. China's royal blood was always replenished from among the people in the most democratic fashion, and a house ruled only as long as it was able to rule.

But with the coming of modern times something happened. When the Manchu throne was empty there were plenty of warlords who wanted it, and certainly one who was able to take it. But the young revolutionary party had also entered the lists. They did not want an empire. They wanted a republic. And the warlords were without reward. They went on, each maintaining his little kingdom, which he changed from time to time as he was driven to do so by actual battle with the new young revolutionary army. Sometimes a warlord would say he was going to subject himself to the government and turn over his army, and be only a general. But none of them quite did it. They always maintained, and do maintain, their own units, which may at any moment be withdrawn.

There has been a new sort of warlord in these modern times, and these are the Communist leaders. Much of Chiang Kai-shek's military energy has been directed against them. They would resent being called warlords, but I use the term with a sense of what it means. I do not despise the Chinese warlord, nor his part in national life. He has been a stronger power for democracy in China than any other. He has been close to the peasantry. He has kept emperors humble and made rich men take thought how much too rich they grew, and a corrupt official was often punished with a rude sort of justice if he oppressed the people too sorely in a warlord's realm. And certainly the manner in which Chu Teh and Mao Tse-tung, the Chinese Communist leaders, have conducted themselves, in the way they have maintained their separate armies, have lived off the rich people, have controlled the regions into which they moved—all this, I say, has been simply historic warlord behavior under a new flag.

107

Well, what has Japan done to this disunited political Chinese life? She has united them all—warlords, Communists, and national government. Nothing but a foreign nation, aggressive to the point beyond endurance, could have driven together all these warring units. Today, for the first time in decades at least, all of China acknowledges one government, and one high military command. It is a tremendous thing to have done. Centuries of peace could not, I believe, have achieved this end. Japan has done it in a few months, a few terrible months, when China has seen that she must unite or die, and she has united herself.

Six years ago I happened to be in Peiping. The Japanese were then bombarding Shanghai, and indeed, beginning the war which is going on today. All about me Chinese of intelligence were saying, "We hope that Japan will not stop the war too soon. War with Japan will unite us as nothing else can." A truce was patched up, however, before long, and the country went on. Today there has been no truce and even the Communists have come under the government flag, after all the bitter years of war against it.

But, it may be asked, "What makes the Chinese and Japanese fight at all?" The answer to that is a long story, and it really is answered only by trying to explain what the Chinese and Japanese are like as people. I often hear Americans say they are afraid of Orientals—their narrow eyes, their yellow skin, their silence. Well, of course that is about as sensible as saying that one is afraid of all white men. There is as much variety among Orientals as there is among us. The Chinese is a totally different creature from the

Japanese, as different as a Frenchman is from a Swede, only more so. The Japanese are right when they complain, as they are doing, that the Chinese dislike them. The Chinese do dislike the Japanese—they more than dislike them, they hate them. If you ask a Chinese why he hates the Japanese he will talk some sort of nonsense about Japanese aggression and all that.

The truth is, the Chinese does not know why he hates the Japanese. His hatred goes back to a time and a source long before there was any aggression. Japanese aggression came because the Japanese grew angry with the Chinese for never agreeing with them about anything and for never wanting to cooperate with them. And the Chinese did not want to cooperate, not because what the Japanese suggested was not good, but just because they did not want to have the Japanese around them or do business with them more than they could help, because they didn't like them. It is all comprehended in that wonderfully true little old verse,

> *I do not like you, Dr. Fell,*
> *The reason why I cannot tell.*

The Chinese and the Japanese were at war ideologically long before they began to fight with guns. All wars, of course, begin in the mind. And the Chinese and the Japanese are at war in their very blood. Their races are different. I laugh when people tell me they cannot tell a Chinese from a Japanese. Put an average Chinese and an average Japanese side by side, and then tell me they look alike. Hair, skin, and color of the eyes are the same, but there any similarity ends.

The Chinese is taller, more slender, and his skull is longer, his eyes are larger, his nose is more defined. He is shapely, his hands and feet are beautiful, with a look of what we call race about them. Universally the Chinese hands are long, slender, and spare, very delicate, the wrist narrow, as the ankle is small. The Chinese body is slender without being thin, and the head is well set and proud. The Japanese is not nearly so handsome. His bones are thick, his figure, though rarely fat, nearly always clumsy and squat. Japanese girls have pretty faces and bad figures, while Chinese girls nearly always have fine figures at least. The Japanese hand and foot are short and square and thick, the nose flat, the eyes small.

Most different of all is the expression on their faces. The Chinese are a gay, undisciplined, merry, happy-go-lucky people, and this shows in their looks. This may not be seen on the faces of Chinese abroad, but then it must be remembered that they are exiles in a strange land and they do not trust strangers. The face of the alien in any country is always closed. But in China one is struck by the merriness of the people. Even the poor people are merry and make the best of what they have. Only in a famine are they downcast, and even then a chance bowl of rice, an unexpected penny, will make them gay. They can endure suffering beyond anything I have ever seen elsewhere.

Once I asked a wretched old man how he could be cheerful over so little, and he said, "Ah, but the wheel turns—the rich of today may be the poor of tomorrow—nothing stays the same." And indeed it does not in China, where a warlord may upset the whole scheme of life in a region five hundred miles square, and where looting is a part of every little war. Once, I was talking with a lady in a rich house, and she told me that none of the rich were ever secure. They knew that the tenants on the lands, the servants in their houses, the clerks in their shops, were always watching them like hungry dogs, waiting for a turn of the wheel of fortune. Three times in her life it had come. What the stock market does for the rich in America, the warlords do for the rich man in China. If one had access to the files of some of our great American banks, one would find that some of the heaviest depositors are Chinese capitalists who prefer to have their funds out of the country so that in an upset something will be left.

But the rich are gay, too. If they may be poor someday, they had better enjoy their good luck, and that sense of the ephemeral quality of life penetrates the Chinese mind. To enjoy what one has without looking into the future is the essence of their philosophy.

Take this war, for instance. As long as I have been mature enough to think, I have known it was inevitable, unless the Chinese took radical steps against it. Some of the accusations the Japanese bring against the Chinese are true. For decades the Chinese children have been calling the Japanese monkeys and little black dwarfs, and they have been taught that the Japanese are their enemies. Japanese colonists living in China have had to suffer great indignity and contempt. For the Chinese is the arch-individualist of the world. If he does not like someone, he wants to spit on him and does.

If he has that person in his power and can do something to him, he does. What the Japanese do not see is that there is a reason for this behavior, and it is that the Chinese simply cannot like them.

When Japan talks about an entente of Oriental nations, she is talking good sense. There ought to be union between the Oriental nations, for it would help them all. But the Chinese do not want an entente, because they do not like the way the Japanese look or behave or smell. They just do not want them around. So whenever they have seen a Japanese on their streets they have let him know they did not like him, and Japanese women in China have stayed in their houses as much as possible. And in a revolution or a civil war scuffle, the Japanese have always been treated more badly by the mobs than were other foreigners—I have seen that with my own eyes. The hatred against the Japanese simply permeates the whole Chinese people.

Why? Well, because they are totally different—so different they cannot understand each other. The Chinese are a gay people, the Japanese are serious. Every Chinese has a sense of humor, and almost no Japanese has. If there were any sense of humor in Japan today they would not be saying the absurd things they are saying, that since China does not like them, they are going to bomb a lot of people and wage a war to make the Chinese change and like them. The Japanese are really hurt because the Chinese do not like them. They remind me of a small girl I once knew who continually fought with her little playmate. I endeavored one day to point out the wrong of this and urged her to re-

form. She was struck with my arguments and at last said
with much energy, "Well, I promise you I won't fight any
more, and if John wants to fight me, I'll knock him down."

The feeling between the Japanese and the Chinese is the
same, only more intense, than that between the French and
the Germans. They are so different that there is no basis for
liking. The Chinese is a born democrat and individualist, he
hates discipline, his idea of a good government is one that
lets him alone—not a bad idea, that—and a dozen rules
against spitting on the floor in a public room will not keep
him from spitting on the floor if he wants to. His sole test
of whether he will do a thing is whether he wants to do it. He
never asks why he does not want to; he does not because he
does not, and that's all there is to it. He hates work but can
work very hard when he likes. He loves ease and quiet and
home and children, and good talk and a great deal to eat and
sleeping in the sun, and good humor everywhere, and above
all things on earth he loves a fine pun or a good joke. He
has lived always in a large country, in a rich country, in a
various country. It is all nonsense to call China poor. The
Chinese have plenty of money. I have seen expenditure on
clothes and feasts and amusements there which passes anything I have seen elsewhere. Wealth is unevenly distributed,
it is true, and yet the middle class live as well as our middle
class, though without our modern improvements. They have
smaller incomes, but their money buys more. And big fortunes are very vast, and no one asks how they were accumu-
lated.

All this immensity, the big country, the crowds of people,

the volatility of mind, lend a certain lightness to the national temperament. If a famine strikes one area, the people simply move into another area. A good many may die on the way, but they always have, and the ones that are left are glad it was not they, and the officials accept the situation as a legitimate means of population control. Life goes on, somehow. If the death rate is enormous, so is the birth rate. China is a great sprawling, glorious, merry, undisciplined creature, immense in everything, and "Live and let live" is her motto.

She is so large that even huge natural catastrophes cannot affect her greatly. An earthquake in Kansu a few years ago about ten times the size of the San Francisco earthquake drew a small notice in the papers one day. A few months ago, when the casualties began to be published from Shanghai, a Chinese gentleman of my acquaintance here in New York read them, apparently undisturbed. "Fifteen thousand —let's see—that is scarcely one in a hundred people—pooh, there will be plenty of Shanghai left," he said.

But there is none of this in the Japanese. If the Chinese are undisciplined, the Japanese are the most disciplined people on earth, not only from without but from within. A sense of duty is the rule by which the Japanese live, a duty narrow as the grave and as inexorable and as harsh. Every movement in his life is controlled by what he has been taught as fit. There is very little rebellion against it. Japanese women are the most limited in the world in their lives, but they accept their limits with graceful, unrepining resignation and make beauty out of what is left to them. The Chinese are unreligious, as any comfortable, rollicking people are unreligious, but the Japanese are religious in a deep, poetic, tragic sense. Religion is a part of all they do. They would have understood our old Puritan fathers, and our fathers would have understood them.

For life has not been as kind to the Japanese as it has been to the Chinese. They live an incredibly difficult existence upon a few mountainous islands. Every grain of rice counts, every leaf of cabbage counts. They know, they accept the fact, that at any moment much of what they have may be swept away by volcano, by tidal wave. Not a year passes that some catastrophe of the sort does not occur in Japan, perhaps many. Out of this sort of life have come two things: a fortitude unsurpassed by any people, and a love of beauty beyond any I know. Much as I love China, I have to acknowledge that the Japanese have made of their small country a perfect jewel of beauty and that China does little to improve her natural gift. Every Japanese house is beautiful, even the very poor somehow create beauty—they love flowers and children and landscape and gardens. Japan is spotlessly clean, beautifully ordered. In some ways it remains to me the most beautiful country I have ever seen. It is one of the contradictions of human nature that with all this beauty which one sees everywhere, among rich and poor alike—the utensils of the poor are beautifully made, the common rice bowl you can buy for a penny is exquisitely lacquered—there is a terrific, dogged, humorless ruthlessness. A soldier may come in from bloody battle, change

115

his clothes, and sit down to enjoy the grace of a flower he has planted in his garden, and feel no conflict in himself. Their very art is compounded of soft cherry blossoms and willows and the short, sturdy, storm-bitten pines on rocky ocean coasts. There is in the Japanese a delicacy and a crudity, a poetic mind and a ruthless heart, which are not united by the only thing that can unite such contradictions, a sense of humor. They are deadly serious, deadly sure of themselves, and unable to see any point of view other than their own.

And this capacity for suffering and hardship which the Japanese have, this frugality and self-discipline and high achievement, makes them feel superior morally. Indeed, they are a people superior morally in many ways. And when people feel superior morally and have no sense of humor to make them tolerant and objective, so that they cannot see themselves and understand others, very soon they begin to think they ought to compel other people to believe as they do and behave as they do. This is what Japan feels today. That reasonableness, which is so lovable in the Chinese, that interest in others, that understanding of all that is human and therefore allowable, is completely lacking in the Japanese.

It has always been fascinating to me to speculate on this endless difference between two neighboring peoples. Why are the Chinese and Japanese so different? It is not enough to say they spring from different races—why have they developed so differently? I feel of course that the explanation is largely geographic. The Chinese are typical of a people

who live in a large country, and the Japanese are the product
of islands, bound about by the sea. It is the same difference
that is between the Americans and the English. The temperament, indeed, of the Chinese and the Americans is
very much alike. And there are likenesses, too, between two
insular peoples, the Japanese and the English. The shape
and size of the country, whether it is an island or a conti-
nent, matters very greatly in the history of a people's development. Largeness, a sense of plenty, little need for real
economy, space in which to move, tend to bring about
humor, individualism, easy going. Limited space, limited
food supply, and a constantly threatening nature and isolation produce a temper somber, serious, and intense.

It is not surprising, therefore, that two neighbors so diametrically different should be at war. It is not a sudden war,
it is a war long expected, and the primary cause of it is not,
I believe, material, but psychological. Of course if Japan
had not been pinched economically, with a growing population, her people might have lived in peace. But if she had
not been geographically constricted she would not have
been Japan. She would have been another country.

Who is going to win the war? Japan may win for the
moment. Or rather, not Japan, but the big guns and the
bombs. Several years ago, when this war was first looming,
I asked an old Chinese gentleman if he feared war with the
Japanese and he replied very tranquilly, "Not at all. Many
people have tried to conquer us and we have always let
them and it has been the end of them. Why, if all the Japanese would move into China we would hardly know it—

we would just wonder where the fleas had come from and for a day or two we would be annoyed. Then we would forget about them."

This has been the traditional Chinese attitude toward foreign conquerors for a good many centuries and it has worked well enough. Pit Chinese against Japanese equally armed and I believe the Chinese would win. But it is not the Japanese who are winning this war; it is the heavy artillery and the bombing planes, and China has never coped with these before.

In the long run, however, it will not be these that decide whether Japan is to rule China. Fighting cannot go on forever on this scale. Victory must come after a while to the question of endurance, and after that to the administration of territory and the carrying on of business. When that time comes the Chinese will have no idea they are a conquered people. They will go on exactly as they always have. They will take off their clothes in public if it is hot and sit in their underwear, and they will spit where they please, both literally and figuratively, and they will not obey rules laid down for them, and when four hundred million people do such things, it will take more people than the Japanese have to persuade them to anything else. Add to this the fact that the Chinese are for centuries used to guerrilla warfare. A single battle lost means nothing to them. Loss of men means nothing—they have plenty of people. Retreat means nothing. Their way of fighting is never to acknowledge or even recognize a victory, but to return again and again to harass, to attack secretly and by devious means, the enemy.

> *When the enemy advances, we retreat!*
> *When the enemy halts and encamps, we trouble them!*
> *When the enemy seeks to avoid a battle, we attack!*
> *When the enemy retreats, we pursue!*

—this is the rule of Chinese war, and the Japanese are not used to it.

In short, eventually the Chinese will conquer the Japanese simply by being themselves. It seems a law of life that the passive persists merely because it is passive and does not spend itself as the more active does. It is the warlike nations that have perished, and it is the pacific nations that have lived long and inherited the earth at last. If China had been a warlike nation in the sense that Japan is today, she would have perished with her contemporary, Rome.

But she is as much alive as ever, and will be, though this particular war be won by Japan. It is possible that sometimes she may even sign treaties and carry out peace conference decisions to a point. But it will mean nothing, for still she will not like Japan. And when a quarter of the earth's people hate Japan, it is a serious hatred, an eternal hatred. Personally, I should not like to be Japan. On the whole, I would rather let China win than win myself, if I were she. If Japan lost, China would be bumptious for a while and then laugh and forget it. But if Japan wins, she has more than a bear by the tail. She has a leviathan.

119

8

We Must Stand Together

My ATTENTION IS always seized on any page by the name of Madame Chiang Kai-shek. Whatever she writes I read because of my long and unchanging admiration for this Chinese woman who in a way is a symbol of all Chinese women, old and new, embodying as she does the integrity, fearlessness, and practical energy of a womanhood as fine as any in the world. I admire Madame Chiang for many reasons, but chief among them is that though she is the daughter of wealth, reared in luxury and privilege and with every advantage that wealth can give, though she was educated abroad and her home was in old international Shanghai, a place far from the struggles of China, with all this she has not chosen the life of shelter and retreat which many sons and daughters of wealth in China have chosen. She has gone as far as she could into the true China, among

Article in Liberty Magazine, *February 15, 1941. Copyright renewed 1968 by Pearl S. Buck.*

the real people, and has spent her energy and her intelligence to do all that she can for them.

And yet I am sorry that she says what she does in her article entitled *Democracy Reaps the Whirlwind*. I am sure she would not say what she has unless she felt it necessary for her. And still I am sure it was not well to say that China is disappointed in the democracies, in what the democracies have done for her, and that after such disappointments the democracies must not be surprised if China deserts the cause of democracy.

I was in China through all the bitter years before 1934 when Japan was fastening her hold upon China in ways so subtle and yet so brazen that one felt the Chinese must know what was happening and one wondered if, incredibly, they did not care. Even the government seemed passive. Then came the days when Japan boldly took Manchuria and China realized what had already happened. She was no more prepared for it than was Europe for Hitler. Yet in the same strange way she knew, she must have known, for we who were living in China knew, that Japan was arming and preparing for conquest. She knew, for Chinese statesmen at Geneva, at Washington, made reports. But China did nothing to prepare herself against aggression. In spite of the fact that across a narrow sea a cruel military power was preparing to invade her, civil war was continued in China and the government occupied itself largely with putting down its agrarian or so-called Communist movement among peasants and students. Thus when Japan actually attacked, China looked desperately for help to the League of Nations.

121

Now the League was in its infancy. It was the weak and childish beginning toward the accomplishment of a noble ideal which I believe the world will one day find to be the only way to solve its international problems. But no ideal can spring full-fledged into reality. Ideals begin as ideas and then go on to be wishes and then hopes. Only slowly can an ideal become a fact. Thus with the League. It was only an idea and scarcely even a wish with enough people to be very far along its way. That China looked toward it for deliverance on a day of fate already fallen simply showed her desperation. Older Chinese understood how powerless the League was for the very reason that nations—and this includes China—had kept it powerless. Every large nation that belonged to the League, including China, did so with the purpose of getting something out of it, not of putting something into it to build it to strength and reality. The League of Nations was only a group of persons, each of whom tried to get as much as he could for his own country and to give as little as he could to others. This is why the League was weak and for this China is exactly as responsible as anybody else. She had no more vision than the rest of the members or than the United States had when she refused to join at all. Therefore no Chinese ought to blame the League's inability to perform in time of crisis. The League had not been built for such performance.

Then China looked to the United States. How many times in those days did I not hear Chinese say confidently that surely Americans would not, out of our friendship for China, allow the Japanese to invade her! I knew they would and must allow it. All nations would and must, even as China has watched the invasions of other countries without any feeling except seeming indifference. China has not herself the record of going to the help of anybody.

Yet the United States was not indifferent to China. In the strongest terms the United States spoke out against Japan's invasion of Manchuria. More she could not do unless China herself did more. China did not. Without preparing even then for what anyone could see would develop into a major war, she pursued, as England did later, a policy of appeasement. Like England's, it failed. Like the English people, once the blow fell the Chinese common people responded with magnificent courage and endurance. They are a people surpassed by none on earth. Betrayed again and again by their rulers, both old and new, by those who should have looked to their welfare and did not, the Chinese people, oppressed by cruel taxation and given surely in return less than any have ever had, quietly determined to resist Japan, with or without weapons. The Chinese people deserve every honor that can be given them, every penny that can be sent to help them, every aid that can be found to preserve their democracy. It is for them that we Americans must work wholeheartedly through all the agencies in which we are working. I am one of a group of Americans who are trying at this moment to raise a million dollars to buy medical supplies to send to China for the millions of people who need them, and there are many other groups working for other Chinese causes.

When I think of China I do not see a young and beautiful

face. I see the indomitable strong brown faces of village men and women who work on the land, of merchants in little shops on village streets and towns—these are the great folk of China. To help them I will do anything, knowing what they are and how they have suffered, not only in times of war but in times of peace. And I am only one American. Throughout the United States there are millions of others. I have letters from many of them, sending dollar bills or a few cents in stamps, all that each can afford out of the little he has. And there are rich Americans who send their thousands and hundreds of dollars in the same spirit.

This friendship of the American people for the Chinese people has gone on for generations. It has been expressed in human lives of devoted American men and women in China as well as in money sent. I think of my own parents who went to China young and spent their lives there and were always poor for China's sake and died there old and still poor and lie buried in Chinese soil. They were not unique. There are many like them. China owes her earliest hospitals and modern schools and institutions for the insane and the blind and lepers to Americans like these, as well as the development of much else in her modern life. I know that Madame Chiang has often expressed her appreciation of these men and women as individuals. But they are more than individuals. There have been too many of them to be only a group of individuals. They were and are Americans and products of our democracy. If they expressed through religion and medicine and education a certain spirit, that spirit was expressed also through our statesmen who steadily and through the years have tried to keep China undivided by foreign powers and free. There is no other country with such a record of disinterested friendship toward Chinese as the United States has, and China herself has no such record toward any other country. China will do well to think twice before turning away from the democracies. For only the democratic countries have bred persons of any reliable international goodwill whatsoever. Even if that goodwill is not quick enough with strong action now, it is nevertheless goodwill.

All this must not be forgotten in the present moment when some Americans have continued to do business with Japan in the materials of war. I cannot approve for any reason such business. There has been almost unanimous disapproval in our country of the sale of goods to Japan which can be used against China. The question has simply been how best to proceed to stop it. Some Americans have wanted to use embargo. Others believe the embargo an act which must be backed by force if it is to be effective and therefore it must be considered as the first step in a possible war to follow, and these Americans have advocated other means to the same end, means no less effective if used, but less dangerous in their results.

But our country is a democracy and we choose democratic ways of deciding our differences even though these ways are slower than the swift decisions of dictators. The United States has not been inactive toward aid for China. It is true that there have been and are individual Americans who have made and are making money from selling gasoline, oil, scrap iron, and other materials of war to Japan. There are also individual Chinese who have made money out of Japan's aggression in China.

It is true, too, that China's war is a war of the democracies, but it has become so only recently as one nation after another has declared for fascism. It did not begin so. It began simply as an aggression by Japan. China and Japan are old enemies. This is not the first war between them. Japan has had her eyes upon China for a long time, and for as long China has known that national weakness might one day be fatal to her. But like the rest of the world she hoped against hope. If she herself did not appraise correctly the character and intentions of Japan, it is not surprising if other nations less directly concerned failed to do so. The League of Nations did not lose Manchuria for China. China lost it because she was not ready to fight for it.

Whether it ought to be or not, the law of nations has been and is that each nation thinks of its own first. There is no nation which is an exception to this or which can cast the first stone at another. The United States, always friendly to China, has had to consider its own people before committing itself to any action that might lead to war. Even now we so consider our aid to Britain. As long as the American people say "anything short of war," it will be short of war. And yet England is closer to us than China, not only geographically but through the ties of blood and history, and Hitler is more of a world menace than Japan is yet. Americans, idealistic as they are and generous as they have been beyond all other peoples in giving their aid to others, can scarcely be expected to assume the role of an all-wise, all-benevolent nation in a world where others are so in such little measure. Humanity progresses together—none is perfect when all are not perfect.

But this is a time for patience with one another and not for recrimination and accusation. Others must be patient with America when prudence and self-interest seem to them our first thought. And we in America must be patient with cries from China and England and Greece and Finland and Poland and Czechoslovakia, from Spain, France, and Belgium and Norway and Denmark and Holland, and all desperate countries who blame us for too little help or for help given too slowly. We must be patient and we must try to help more quickly.

I can understand and sympathize with the feelings of Madame Chiang, a sensitive woman and one overburdened with the sorrows of her own people. She does much but no one can do enough, and it is only natural that the too sad heart should cry out in anger. But let us remember that not out of anger or even resentment against sorrow should fateful decisions be made.

The decision of China against democracy would be very fateful indeed. It would be especially so at this moment when between the democracies there is developing, in the slow, strong, sure way that is the people's way, the determination to stand together against tyranny. I should not like to see China, the country that I love next to my own, the country that I know even better than my own, left out of that union. The world of the future needs China as one of the victors in

127

this struggle between freedom and tyranny, not as one of the vanquished. Above all other nations the Chinese belong, by their history and by their nature, with the democracies. And if the Chinese people are given their choice today, they will choose democracy.

9

The Secret of China's Victory

IN THESE DAYS OF extraordinary events there is one which overtops all others. It is the fact now slowly dawning upon us that China is actually winning her part of this world war, that is, the war with Japan. I say slowly dawning upon us, because in China's usual colossal silent fashion the great fact has been allowed to stand for itself. She has not wasted money on propaganda. In a day when propaganda is openly announced as one of the important weapons of modern warfare, it is characteristic that China has not bothered about it. She has been always indifferent to what people thought about her and she still is, except for a fringe of overmodernized and sensitive persons who, having lived much abroad, have lost the understanding of their own country.

To this frantic fringe of her own people China also pays no heed. She has not even made known her victories abroad. In a recent article the Chinese writer Lin Yutang gives in

Speech in Cleveland, Ohio, July 10, 1941.

some detail the names and accounts of important battles won by the Chinese, of which we have scarcely or never heard. Newspapers did not report them and there was no noise about them anywhere else. They were not unduly emphasized even in China—that is, with their extraordinary good sense, the Chinese do not take a battle for a war. If a battle is won, it is one step forward; if it is lost, it is one step backward in the long struggle. They give heed in that struggle only to the trend of the whole. Why, therefore, announce the incident and mislead, perhaps, many persons thereby?

None of China's secret of victory, therefore, lies in clever propaganda, for of that she has none. The world has known little of that grim, enormous struggle which now for more than four years has been going on upon Chinese soil. Those of us who were bent on keeping up with it have had to search for information, dig for it like treasure in every source we know.

But big news is today beginning to come out of China, not in headlines or in radio announcements. It is coming out with a sort of compelling force of its own, like a great light in the western sky. There are few details, less description, no embellishment. There is not even a statement. There is simply becoming apparent a mighty fact: China is winning the war. It is a typically Chinese sort of winning. There has been no one great battle. I doubt there will ever be one. There have been no spectacular weapons. Simply by the steady, massive pressure of her determination not to yield, China is winning the war.

The Secret of China's Victory

How is she winning? What are her secrets? To answer these questions I must take you back nine years. The first overt act of this war now spreading over the world was the seizure of Manchuria by Japan. We all know now that the series of violent and dishonorable acts of aggression which has made this second world war unparalleled in the history of human disgrace began with that act. We all see it now but few saw it then. China saw it. I happened nine years ago to be living in China and I heard on every hand the wonder that the Western nations did nothing about this act of Japan's. "In pure self-defense," the Chinese exclaimed, "Europe and the United States should forbid this act!" The United States did, as we know, express disapproval but was not supported in that disapproval by Britain, who then was beginning the appeasement policy which was the road she chose to follow almost to its precipitous end. The League of Nations sent a commission to investigate the Manchurian situation. The Chinese watched the work of this committee with painful anxiety. Manchuria proved to be the grave of the League. The feebleness of its actions there showed to the world its fundamental weakness and it never breathed again as a living thing.

As for China, she accepted the belief that Japan would one day attack her. What, we all asked, would China do to prepare? So far as we could see, she did nothing. I lived in those days in Nanking, then the capital of new China, and I had every opportunity to discover what Chinese leaders were doing and what the people were thinking. There were acute intelligent perception of the situation and very accurate

131

prognostications of the future, but the most curious preparations for war that a Western mind can imagine.

Today in our own country we are preparing for war. Our industries are swinging into vast military production. Our manpower is being mobilized. The mind of the nation is being hewn and shaped toward the one aim of defense for war.

But nine—eight—seven—six years ago, I saw a huger nation than ours face certain invasion in a very different fashion. China had no heavy artillery but she made no effort, or very little, to get any, and certainly none to make any. She could make guns and light artillery, but nothing bigger. She had few airplanes. Her air force was weak not only in planes but in personnel. The Chinese common man can be taught something about machinery, but the spoiled sons of the rich and the intelligentsia are almost childish in their lack of ability to understand and handle machinery, and most of her air force were these young men. We who were watching at close range in those days gave way at times to secret despair over the things we heard and saw around airfields. No apparent effort was made to improve the situation until Madame Chiang herself took over the air force in an attempt at least to rid it of corruption in connection with buying airplanes from abroad. No attempt was made to produce airplanes. It was as much as the Chinese could do, apparently, to assemble them when they arrived.

China's navy was nonexistent—a few old ships, the best of them far behind the requirements of a modern battleship. Her army was an unknown quantity. Chiang Kai-shek's personal troops were said to be first-rate, but he would not,

of course, throw them into the battle front. Other generals
and warlords had their own armies and there was some sort
of a Communist army. The great question was, would these
armies unite—could they unite? Certainly Chiang Kai-shek
himself could not unite them, for he had been carrying on
a civil war for years against the Communists. So far as
could be seen, no effort was made to unite them as attack
grew nearer, day by day.

Moreover, even if they were united, what of the army
leadership? It has long been known that the Chinese common soldier is not to be matched for courage, flair, and
endurance. But the leaders were weak. German army advisors were used for many years in China, and they always
said the same thing—the Chinese common man made a
magnificent soldier, but the stuff out of which leaders were
made seemed poor. The traditional weakness of China has
been in her upper classes, and her great strength that these
classes were so small in proportion to the rest of the population. There are reasons for this weakness which time fails me
to give now, for they are many. Chief of them, however, is
the traditional Chinese idea that the rich man and the
educated man cannot work at anything practical and maintain his self-respect. The hardships of this war are breaking
that tradition to bits today, but its existence for centuries
has done damage in Chinese life. Nowhere did it do more
damage than in the army, for out of the classes that should
have provided captains and generals there came weak,
pampered, often cowardly young men.

With such prospects China faced the most serious attack

of her history. For though China had been attacked before by aggressive peoples, she had never been conquered, even though in a military sense she lost. We all know that whoever tried to conquer China was in the end conquered by absorption into that vast and tolerant nation. But she had always been attacked in the past by people inferior to herself. Was Japan inferior to China? It was difficult to say she was. I do not feel that Americans give to the Japanese their full due as human beings. It shows ignorance to dismiss Japanese people by the common phrase that they are a lot of imitative monkeys. This is not true. Though I disapprove completely Japan's militarism, I must acknowledge that the Japanese people among whom I have at times lived are courteous, and civilized as few peoples are on this earth, and that in their fashion they live up to their national ideals better than most are able to do. They are not imitative—they are intelligent and inquiring and do not have the stupid pride which forbids learning what is good from others. What they learn, moreover, is not copied wholesale; it is adapted and changed to suit Japan, so that while Japan is modernized, she has kept in an extraordinary degree her own peculiar quality. The Japanese people are clean, religious, and beauty-loving, and they are among the bravest people on earth. Strong and self-disciplined—disciplined, too, by a severe natural environment which at any moment threatens earthquake and tidal waves—they are the last people on earth to regard as decadent. Japan is a formidable foe.

All this was the more dismaying to those of us who loved China. Japan had not only army, navy, and air force, far superior to those China possessed, but her people were strong. China had never before been attacked by a strong modern people. Could she absorb the Japanese as she had absorbed the Mongols and the Manchus? Many wise heads feared she could not. China herself made, apparently, no preparations.

And yet in their own way the Chinese were making preparations. First, there was gathering a great deep determination among the people that they would resist aggression, with or without weapons. Second, this resistance must mean union, and they proceeded to become unified, not by any official proclamation from above or propaganda. No, the people determined on unity. Warlords who had been bitterly against the government now gave allegiance to the government. The Communists, thousands of whom Chiang Kai-shek had killed, now voluntarily swore loyalty to him so long as he led resistance against this common enemy. It was an extraordinary and magnificent popular unification which we here in America ought to realize for our own encouragement. The differences between Chiang Kai-shek and his followers and the Communist leaders and their followers were as grave and as irreconcilable as the differences between the black and white races in our own country. But for the sake of the defense of China those differences were put aside. Can we, too, put aside the grave and unjust discrimination now being shown to colored Americans on every hand in order that we may have unity in our country at this dangerous hour? The Chinese have shown us what can be done by a people determined for true democracy.

There were other preparations in China for a long war of defense. Universities prepared to carry on their work by building or renting buildings thousands of miles away in the interior beyond any possibility of invasion. This began as long as two years before the actual invasion. Other universities are carrying on in inland temples, caves, and dugouts. The Chinese government prepared its defense by telling Chinese students to continue their education and not to waste themselves by joining the army. They would be wanted for more important, more constructive work than war in the future of the nation.

Not only the universities but as many as possible of China's industrial plants moved inland. Not only these, but an enormous number of Chinese moved inland, people of every class and occupation, a migration unparalleled in the world's history. This was their preparation for war. It was not cowardice or fear. It was preparation.

In like manner Chiang Kai-shek prepared his campaign for a series of masterly moves, in no Chinese sense retreats, designed to lead the enemy inland to a point where the Chinese armies, strengthened and massed, would take their stand.

Today, after more than four years, the situation is briefly this: Japan has scattered her forces over a large territory which she is unable to control from sheer size and the hostility of its people, and she cannot proceed farther. In ancient times China built the great wall against invaders. Today five million men, with ten million in training and reserve, are holding a fighting line twenty-eight hundred miles long. Against them Japan has not been able to prevail. Distance and terrain forbid serious attack. Behind this living wall of men, still armed only with rifles and light artillery, free China grows in strength as she prepares to take back the land. Industrial cooperatives are working, roads are being made for motor vehicles, land being reclaimed for food, agricultural improvements of all sorts are going on. China is building for the future while she resists the present. The time will come, and perhaps sooner than we think, when a discouraged Japanese army will be pushed back into the sea.

It would be folly today to paint any human picture too bright. There are Chinese traitors, Chinese opportunists, Chinese profiteers. These are being dealt with by death when possible, by scorn and ignoring otherwise. The Chinese, while seeming to tolerate evil, are not ignorant of it. There is much allowance for human nature, but terrifying vengeance when it becomes a menace to the life of the people. There is a fifth column in China, there are local puppet governments in occupied territory—none has any real power.

It is true that in occupied China the people are in desperate circumstances. Already impoverished farmers are being compelled to raise opium for the Japanese. They are taxed to an incredible degree, and these profits go for the most part not to the Japanese government but to local

Japanese officers and governors. These Chinese are the real sacrifices to the war. And yet they, too, go on with steady secret resistance. Guerrillas harass the Japanese armies and no one can overstate the importance of guerrillas in this war. The people harass by noncooperation, there is no real pacification. In homes throughout occupied China the Chinese flag is hanging, the songs of free China are sung, and the sure day of independence awaited.

No one who knows China doubts its coming. With our help it will come more quickly, but with or without us it will come. The vitality of the Chinese people guarantees it. In this vitality lies China's secret of victory, the vitality of a people accustomed to freedom for thousands of years. For China never has been much governed from above. Her real government has been local, village government, administered by strong common men and women who farmed the land and bought and sold food and goods over the counters of small shops.

Whence comes this human vitality? On a day like this it is important to know. France fell like a house of paper. China, with none of the equipment France had for defense, after four years of war against a modern nation stands stronger today than ever.

The vitality comes of course out of the Chinese common people, her farmers, her merchants, her teachers and students, her laborers and artisans, and out of men and women equally. Most of the people in China are just everyday folk. I know we like to think of strange and splendid Oriental luxury but I assure you there is much more of that sort of thing here than there is in China. The so-called upper classes are certainly smaller in China than anywhere else, and even so are peculiarly fluid. Families rise from the common ranks and return to them with amazing rapidity. There are no "old" Chinese families in our American sense, and yet in another sense all Chinese families are old. A peasant's family may have been a thousand years upon a certain piece of land and be there still, though in the long space his family in its branches may have spread into very high places. But however high these branches went, always the roots remained upon the earth, and however distant from it some members of the family went, earth was and is always looked upon as the home of man, and no family is content unless it has its deepest, oldest roots in land. Their earth belongs thus to the Chinese people and from it they draw their sense of solidarity and reality. There is no Chinese, whether he lives actually upon land or not, who is not in one sense or another close to the land. His material fortunes depend upon the harvests of rice and silk and vegetables and vegetable oils and animal products, and his spiritual nature is fed by nature and the seasons more even than by religion. The whole Chinese year is framed upon season and harvest and the moon, to which only recently have been added the dates of national heroisms.

This closeness to the land and its life has made the Chinese people earthy and practical in their attitude toward life, and has given them the sources of their ability to endure.

This is the first secret of her vitality. The second is the fluidity of Chinese society, which in its democracy allows a man to rise from low place to high regardless of his birth. The fact that in China there is no such thing as a "station in life" has produced a hopefulness in the spirit of the people that can be had in no other way. There is always chance for change, for improvement, for freedom of movement, and so there is nothing dull or static in the temper of the people. Anyone who goes to China is struck with the independent bearing of even the poorest Chinese. He looks a free man because he is a free man and knows he is. He is accustomed to self-government and to responsibility for himself and his family. He knows he is free to improve himself and his fortunes. He is less dependent, therefore, on leadership than any average man in the world. If he has inspired leadership, he can accomplish miracles, not through compulsion, but because he is wise enough to value such leadership. If he has poor leadership, he manages well enough without it, being sensible and resourceful in himself. I cannot sufficiently praise the common men and women of China. The vitality of the nation springs from them. When men or families depart too far from that source, vitality leaves them and they know it, and they renew themselves again by marriage to peasants or by voluntary return to the land. This too means fluidity in the social system and consequently a democratic point of view.

Third, the Chinese social system has given its members an extraordinary amount of individual security through the family system. Nothing so weakens the individual in a nation as a feeling of economic insecurity and personal loneliness. In China the individual is neither insecure nor lonely. His family stands with him and for him, to his remotest cousin. The family cares for the old, the sick, the bereaved, the orphan. Whatever its disadvantages—and there are not a few—at least the big family system provides security for the individual. This I believe accounts in large measure for the universal gaiety of the Chinese people. They are gay, not as children are gay out of ignorance, but as very wise people are gay, who have learned how few are the important things in life and how, therefore, to laugh at all else if they have food to eat and their own people beside them.

Fourth, the vitality of the Chinese springs from their rich sense of humor. Laughter is but another proof of their vitality. Only vital people laugh easily and often as the Chinese do.

I suppose it is only natural that their sense of humor should be strong when of all peoples they possess, partly because they are so old, so fine a sense of proportion in life, since the sense of humor is founded upon the sense of proportion.

One of the greatest pleasures of living in China is the ordinary talk on the streets and in homes and the wit and joking which go on in all the ordinary affairs of life. I could never get anywhere on time because there were so many interesting and amusing conversations to listen to—not private conversations, but passages between perfect strangers, perhaps, as they did their business in open-air tea shops or open-front shops. Everybody listens to everything and the scene often took on the aspects of a play—

with the passing crowd the audience, and the others impromptu actors. How often have I not stopped to listen to and to see such scenes; peddlers from the north bringing grass cloth south to sell, or vendors, or traveling marionette men, jugglers, and mimics. On summer nights what scenes are the streets! The houses are too hot to sleep in, and people move out on the street to sing, to talk, to tell each other tales, to fall asleep at last under the stars or the moon. Blacksmith shops open to the street, their furnaces backgrounds for the sooty figures forging plowshares and kitchen knives, tailor shops with figures bent beside flickering little oil lamps—and everywhere ready talk and witty persiflage and salty humor with always a bit of friendly wit especially for the foreigner!

I once passed an old man watching two Americans playing tennis, not very well, under a broiling August sun. After he had watched innumerable balls driven into the net and laughed for some time in silence, he was moved to sympathy with their efforts and bawled at them, "Sirs, why don't you take down the net?" This was his sense of proportion at work. I don't know that it was wrong. Why is so much energy in midsummer spent upon getting a ball over a net? I have often wondered myself.

To be a ready purveyor of jokes is to have a passport anywhere in China. White men, and my own father among them, have saved their lives by a quick joke and turned an angry mob to laughing good humor. Laughter is a revivifying force and a people who can laugh often and easily is a people fitted for endurance.

Fifth, I put as one of the Chinese secrets their respect for age. China is a heavenly place for the old, and therefore for everybody, since sooner or later everybody is old. In China, and I assure you I speak the truth, except for a few Westernized ones, women will tell their true age with pride because their social status advances with age. The aged are not only cared for and revered in their families, but the Chinese people actually believe that old people can teach other people something merely because they have lived longer. Old people therefore are not waste in the population. They are useful and know themselves useful and so are self-respecting to the end of their lives. This, too, contributes to gaiety and a good time. Old people are the most delightful people in the world when they feel secure and self-respecting, and China is full of merry old people who do not long to be young, who don't want to be young, and who don't need to be young. China values and uses her old, and they contribute their vitality to her because they are not depressed by discouragement and fear.

I could, if I liked, point out many weaknesses in Chinese society. They are there; you would see them the very first day you went to China as a stranger. The real Chinese make no effort to conceal their weaknesses. You would go on seeing them and sometimes they would make you impatient. But I do not feel these weaknesses worth talking about today, because whatever they are it is evident that they have not been sufficient to make the Chinese people weak or decadent or supine. The oldest most civilized nation in the world and at the same time the least modern in the

Western mechanized material sense, China is, I believe, the strongest nation in the world today, solely because the spirit of her people is so strong. They have not only endured as a nation for thousands of years beyond their contemporaries in ancient Egypt and Greece and Rome, but they are alive today after four years of modern warfare. The Chinese have found a way to live that keeps them alive and perpetually renewed and now are actually maintaining themselves against a modern nation. It is a spectacle, a wonder, a miracle.

You may ask, why if China has this strength in herself, why should we help her? The Chinese will muddle through somehow, you say, and meanwhile there is England.

Without wanting to take a dollar away from England, I reply that to send England relief is not enough. We must let China know that we are her friends, that we see and appreciate her valor. We must strengthen our friendship with China. The Far East is very near to us now and will be nearer in the future. It is useless to defeat the Axis in Europe if the Axis is not defeated in Asia. It is danger to us if China becomes the powerhouse for Japan, an Axis power, or for Hitler himself, now pushing toward Asia. The events of the last few days since Germany has declared war on Russia only prove how high a value Hitler puts upon Asia. Be sure he understands to the full the value of that part of Asia that is China, strong in its people, fertile in its soil, rich in its resources.

Yet China's very size and strength of character make an excuse among some Americans as to why we should not help the Chinese. China is so big, they say, there are such millions of Chinese—England by comparison becomes small and tangible and within the reach of our aid. But this surely is sheer ignorance. England is not a little besieged island off the coast of Europe. England is only part of a mighty empire, with millions more English subjects than there are Chinese in China. There are three hundred and fifty million English subjects in India alone—India, that storehouse of riches for the British empire! There are millions more of British allies in Africa, in Canada, in Australia and New Zealand. Those countries are all pouring their wealth of men and materials and equipment for modern warfare into England. And we, too, pour our strength into England, while to China we give almost nothing—even now after four years of war we are actually giving more aid to Japan than to China in war materials, in spite of embargoes. We are trying to raise five million dollars for Chinese relief. We once gave eleven millions for relief to Japan after a simple earthquake. The real truth is that the Chinese are bearing the whole brunt of the world war in the Far East and bearing it alone. England has done nothing for her and we have done worse than nothing in helping Japan. With far less territory than England has at her command, with far less equipment for war, with less of everything except splendid morale, China fights on alone.

We want China at the peace table with us at the end of this war because of the great common sense of the Chinese and because of their practical shrewdness. They will help us not to repeat the fatal mistakes of the Treaty of Versailles.

They will help us not to waste time and build future wars by any such punitive nonsense. Their aim will be a treaty that will provide as quickly as possible for a return to peace and prosperity for all nations including the enemy. The Chinese make good Christians not because they get converted from anything to anything but because the extreme good sense, as expressed in the Golden Rule which is the basis of Christianity, the product of another old race, is natural to the Chinese anyway. A good Chinese makes a good Buddhist, or Catholic, or Presbyterian or Baptist or Methodist because he is a good Chinese first and glorifies whatever he chooses to become.

The Chinese are the sort of people therefore who should be given every aid to continue their existence as a free people in the world. They have held out bravely for four years, and with far fewer resources than England has, they will struggle on against far greater odds.

And we must help them, not only for victory, but that in the peace to come, the peace of which we dream and for which we hope, the Chinese can help more than any other people upon this earth to make it a lasting peace. They have proved that a people can exist for four thousand years because they live and believe in peace. The warlike nations, the civilizations that have been built upon militarism are dead. China, the nation that has never fought an aggressive war, is living today, and China has something to teach us all about peace as the foundation for long life. We cannot spare China from the world of the future.

10

The Unity of China

I T HAS BEEN A MATTER of insufficient wonder that the Chinese have existed without stop for four thousand years. They are a monument so enormous that we are blinded by its very size. Were there a statue or a temple or a palace that had existed so long and today was still strong and in use, that would be a marvel small enough to see and comprehend and everyone would exclaim over it. But here is a nation, the largest nation in the world today, having a great territory and a fifth of the world's population, a nation still medieval in many of its aspects, a nation proceeding at its own individual rate of development un-regarding the pace of the world about it, who nevertheless, when attacked by all the aggressive force of the modern military machine upon which science has spent its greatest effort, continues to live and to be, and without any obvious material superiority beyond extent of territory is today actually stronger than the day the war began. This is China

Speech before United China Relief, New York City, May 21, 1941.

and China is in a very significant and important sense the Chinese people and their land.

Who are these Chinese? They are for the most part plain people. A smaller percent of China's population belongs to the so-called upper classes than is true of any other nation. Eighty-five percent of the Chinese are rural— small farmers who depend on the land and who live in little villages. Of the remaining fifteen percent another ten percent, approximately, belongs to the small merchant class. There remains only five percent to include the wealthy, the intellectuals, and the governing groups.

The plain people, therefore, are China. When they make articulate their demands, the nation speaks. Thus when they demanded war of resistance against Japan, war was declared, even though the leaders of the government were well aware how meager were the tools of defense. And yet they, too, knew that the best defense was the spirit of the common people.

This spirit deserves examination today, when nations are toppling from dry rot within. Here in China is a nation that does not topple. It has not yielded either to its aggressive enemy or to its own appeasers. Medieval in many of its social institutions and certainly in its material, mechanical, and industrial development, it has at least not fallen. Without an adequate tax system, without a well-defined modern form of democratic government, midway, indeed, in its own slow political and social revolution, when all techniques were in the experimental stage, China has had to pause to fight a defensive war. But some deep unifying

principle in the people has held, without any of these techniques. In spite of dissension at many points, in spite of
venality in high places, their essential unity still holds. A
less sentimental people does not exist. Of corruption where
there should be none they are well aware, and at the proper
time they will reckon with it. It is typified by an experience
I once had in a small inland Chinese town. There was a
temple in that town notorious for the corruption of its
priests. But the plain people continued to worship at the
temple though they perfectly knew the evil life of the
priests, so at variance with the religion for which the temple
stood. One day, being in the temple, I watched an elderly
gentleman in a patched coat come in to pray and to burn
incense to one of the gods. When he had finished I asked
him if he would explain something to me as a foreigner. He
replied very courteously that he would gladly do so if he
could. Whereupon I asked him, "How is it that many good
people continue to worship at this temple when it is well
known that its priests are evil?" To which he answered with
surprise, "But the people come to worship the gods. Are the
gods in whom they believe to be rejected because a few men
are evil?"

The Chinese people are unified and have been unified for
centuries, else how could China have lasted as a nation
and a civilization? Her political unity has been her weakest,
because the people value it least. Westerners value it highly,
but that is a difference from the Chinese. All the unity essential between human beings the Chinese have. They are
of one general race. They are unified by centuries of history

experienced in common, when their unity of spirit outlasted and finally conquered every conqueror who came upon them with superior armies. They are unified in their religions, none of their three religions excluding belief in the others, so that without conflict of any sort a man may be at the same time a Confucian, a Taoist, and a Buddhist. They have similar if not identical social customs over the widest area in the world and a cuisine varied but mutually known and enjoyed. They have a common written language, the same literature and art, and a common spoken language, which, excluding a few dissimilar dialects, is spoken by more persons to speak one language than any other in the world, with the possible though doubtful exception of English.

What better basis can there be therefore for the further progress of democracy than the Chinese now have? A huge population of plain people accustomed to self-government, used to responsibility for their lives, rooted in individualism and in the common life, there could scarcely be material less fitted for Fascist domination. If the Western democracies fail to comprehend this fact, they will be the losers. An enormous political ally awaits them. What waste not to use it, what ignorance not to know even that it is there!

It is wise and right, therefore, at this significant moment, when nations are declaring themselves for or against freedom for their peoples, that we, the people of the United States, should by our sympathy and our aid, declare our friendship for the people of China.

11

China

WHAT IS IT GOING to mean that men from America are pouring into China? One must think in two ways; first, what it will mean to Americans to be sent so suddenly to China with necessarily very little preparation for going there. But I think, too, of the Chinese—I can see Chinese looking at you who are Americans. They look at you with gratitude, I know, but with doubt and wonder, too. If you feel strange to be landed in a country you have never seen, and perhaps have even heard of only a little, whose language you cannot understand or speak, whose food is unknown to you, whose people are not yours, then remember that the Chinese feel as strange to have you there. They will be asking each other, "What shall we do with these, Americans who have come to help us? What do they like to eat and how do they live and work and amuse themselves? Will they

Expanded from a talk to American men about to leave to serve as soldiers in China during World War II.

151

like us? How can we make them understand what we want
to say?"

I should like to say at the outset, before you ever set foot
on Chinese soil, that you will find the Chinese like you before you come. Chinese have long liked Americans. Before
you came to China there were many other Americans who
have made your way easy for you—some of then were missionaries, some of them teachers, many were doctors and
nurses and businessmen. By and large these Americans
have behaved well in China. They have, more than any
other white persons, recognized the Chinese as their equals,
and the Chinese, being a proud and highly civilized people,
have been quick to feel and appreciate this. When you
get to China, therefore, you have your welcome waiting for
you. What you do with it after that is up to you. You may
during your stay there make the Chinese feel you are another typical American and they will like you, or you may
make them feel that you are an exception to a pleasant race.

This might be difficult for you as a stranger who does not
know Chinese customs and feelings if the Chinese were a
complex and exacting people. Fortunately they are not. They
are easygoing, full of fun and good humor, always ready
to laugh, hot-tempered when they are provoked, quick to
forget a quarrel when it is over. They have few taboos and
less formality. They never blame a foreigner any more
than they would a child for breaking a rule of politeness.
They are wonderfully ready to make allowances for the
stranger. But you must not mind if they laugh at you—
they will not mind if you laugh at them, too. Thus they may

152

grin with delight over your looks, which are so different from theirs, but it will be with good-natured and frank amusement. They will not stab you behind the back. The Chinese are not a treacherous people, and once you are friends with them and they know you like them and are their friends, they will stick by you through anything. Loyalty is a national characteristic of the Chinese.

Here are a few things which the Chinese hate—bad temper, surliness, grouchiness, a blow upon the person, an uneven, touchy disposition, excitability, an attitude of superiority because you are a white man, disrespect to women, bossiness. Here are a few things they love—cheerfulness, a ready laugh, ability to see a joke even when it is on you, frankness, human equality, respect for women, love of children, calmness and seeming unhurriedness even when you are in a hurry, courtesy to all—not formal courtesy, but just pleasantness. Why should I say that Chinese hate or love these things? It is what all of us hate and love. In other words, in general, behave in China as you would in your own country, and you will get along very well, provided you are the ordinary, decent, good-natured individual which most Americans are.

Still, I would not be quite fair to you if I did not stress one or two things which you ought to know. The attitude toward women in China is different from ours in America. Chinese women in some ways are more free than they are here in America—that is, they do some things which American women don't yet do. They are in the army, for instance, and they fight side by side with the guerrillas, and you will find them in positions in China which American women have not yet reached. But in their relations with men they are not so free as they are in America. You must not put your arm as casually around a Chinese girl as you do an American girl—not, at least, until you are sure just who she is. There are Chinese girls in cabarets and places of amusement who are used to these ways and who will think of them as simply part of their job. But the average Chinese girl will be insulted if you touch her, or will take you more seriously than you probably want to be taken. I should say that the average girl in America could measure your gesture—how much or how little it meant—but that the average Chinese girl would think you meant the worst, in which case you might have an angry family on your hands and a minor international incident; or if she capitulated, she would expect marriage or at least an establishment for life. For ordinary purposes, therefore, the American soldier should be very sure that the girl is of the proper class for the nature of his advances.

Beyond this, you will find the modern Chinese girl, especially if she speaks English, a friendly, interesting, though perhaps somewhat shy person. She is still a little shy of social equality with men, for she is only recently out of the times which kept men and women apart, except in the family, and she is more than usually shy with a foreigner because she has heard that American men and women are very free with each other and she is perhaps a little fearful. In general, it is wise to keep hands off the Chinese girls, unless you know your girl very well indeed.

Chinese children you may thoroughly enjoy. They are friendly, jolly little souls, delighted with anything you can do to amuse them. They may surprise you with the number of their dirty faces—the average busy Chinese mother washes her children's faces morning and night and what happens between she considers none of her business. But nobody in China sees a child's dirty face—it is taken for granted that if children are having a good time they will be dirty. Do not be surprised if at first the Chinese children are afraid of you. The truth of it is that they will be startled, to say the least, by the way you look. Many of them will never have seen anybody whose hair and eyes were not black and whose skin was not brown like their own. I suppose that most Chinese children consider the way they look to be the way all normal human beings look as a matter of course. Consider, then, what it would be like suddenly to see an outsize individual, in strange clothes, with blue eyes and light hair, a faded, whitish skin and enormous features! This, if you think a minute, will explain the sudden look of fearful wonder in a Chinese child's eyes when he first looks at you.

You will see the same look sometimes in a farmer's face or a woman's. The reason for this is that just as our mystery stories and movies have made Orientals the villains, so Chinese mystery and murder stories have made red-haired, blue-eyed, white-skinned men the villains. It is natural to every country to make the stranger, the foreigner, a villain. In short, when you don't understand something about people in China, think about people in America and you will understand. And usually that fear will fade away very soon if you can say you are American. Perhaps the first Chinese phrase you ought to learn is, *"Wo shih Mei-kuo ren,"* or, "I am an American."

Where will you land in China? I wonder. If I knew that, I could tell you what you would see and what you could find and what to expect. But there is no way in which you or I can tell where you will land, so I shall have to tell you what you will find depending upon whether you will be in the city or in the country. Let us begin with cities, for surely you will see some cities in so crowded a country as China.

Chinese cities are of two kinds, those which have been modernized and those which remain as they have been for centuries. The largest of the modern ones are Shanghai, Tientsin, Nanking, Hong Kong, Canton, Hankow, Peiping —now, alas, all in Japanese hands. You may not see them for a while yet. I need therefore waste little time on them, though they would not need much time in any case. You could behave there very much as you would in New York or London because the atmosphere would be cosmopolitan. Many Americans and Europeans have lived in those cities a lifetime before this war without ever learning to speak or understand a word of Chinese, or eating any Chinese food or going into any Chinese house, or indeed even speaking to any Chinese except a servant, just as, if you were an American in the prewar days, you could have lived in Paris without touching the life of any French person. All you would need in such cities is a guidebook to tell you which were the best hotels and where you would find the movies and the cabarets, the race track and the clubs, and there are—or were—plenty of such guidebooks.

But most cities in China are Chinese, and it is much more likely that you will see these, at least at first. Some of them will be large and some small, but all of them will have certain characteristics in common, as cities do anywhere, but especially where, as in China, they have continued as centers of human life for generations. Many of these cities will be inside an encircling wall, so that you will enter the city through a great gate, open in the daytime but shut at night. There are at least four such gates—east, west, north, south—and there may be others. Often there is a gate called Tai Ping Men, or Gate of Peace, which means that it is an extra gate used for escape in time of war, when all the regular gates might be barred or even in the hands of the enemy.

Once inside the city you will find that the main streets run between the gates, with less important ones branching off into innumerable alleys and lesser ways. You will be impressed by three things: first, that the streets are narrow; second, that they are dirty; and third, that they are crowded. All three are true. Chinese cities are old and, as in old cities in Europe or England, the streets are narrow, built long ago not for automobiles and modern traffic but for sedan chairs and wheelbarrows, and caravans of donkeys and for pedestrians with or without burdens. The gutters are defective if there are any gutters, and because China has not considered plumbing an essential to civilization, people often throw water and garbage out of their doors, just as they used to do in the old days—not so old, either —in our cities and in English cities. Modern Chinese cities, of course, have wide, paved streets and as good sewers as we have in any American city. But we are speaking of the Chinese cities you will probably see the most.

The streets will be lined with shops open to the crowds in the daytime and boarded up at night. At the sides of the street there will be markets of all kinds of vegetables and fruits and sweets and foods and meats. If it is summer, there will be plenty of flies and those flies you must treat very seriously indeed. They are not the comparatively innocent American variety. Since China is an old and populous country, germs, as well as people, have flourished there for centuries, and there has not yet been established a complete national public health system. People sell what they like as they like, of course, and the buyer takes the risk.

The result of this, of course, is that either Chinese people have developed an immunity to many of the diseases which kill the white man all too easily, or else it is that the weak die while the strong survive. They have also developed a sort of wisdom through experience which makes them avoid cold water in their stomachs and they drink hot tea instead, and indeed avoid cold food in general. Boiling heat kills most germs. It kills cholera and dysentery germs and most of the intestinal troubles which harass the white man in China. You should therefore follow one very simple rule there—eat nothing that is not so hot that you know it is only recently off the fire. You can learn to drink hot tea as the Chinese do, and do not yield to the temptation of a fruit that cannot be peeled or cut before your eyes. It is better not even to use a utensil that has not been scalded with boiling hot water. Avoid sweets and cakes except in freezing winter weather, when they will be safe enough. Wash your hands with soap and water before you eat. And do not allow yourself to be bitten by mosquitoes.

These few rules are enough to keep you well in China. I have from childhood traveled much there, eating always entirely off the country and enjoyed it all without once falling ill simply by observing these rules. But to break one once may be enough to undo all your previous care.

You may want to buy something in the shops you see along the Chinese streets. It is customary for the shop-keeper to ask about twice as much as the article is worth. If you pay what is asked, he will not respect you for it. If you argue him down too much, he would prefer not to sell to you at all. If you pay about half to two-thirds what he asks, he will admire you and enjoy the transaction. But above all, keep good-humored throughout. In China it is a sign of bad breeding to grow heated over a purchase, whether it is made successfully or not. If you have learned the Chinese coinage, you will not need language—you can simply put down your money bit by bit. Do not put down at first what you are really willing to pay, but less, so that you can have something to compromise with and come up a little—so as to make the shopkeeper feel you are willing to meet him halfway. He will then come down a little to meet you, and you will arrive at a common point where you can agree on the price. Thus you part friends.

Yet it is true that China is as full of human nature as any other country, and of course there will be people there who think only of themselves and what they can get as profit out of your being there. You have this misfortune: you are paid in American dollars, which just now are fabulously valuable in China. China is not a poor country as countries go, but she is poorer than the United States, and besides she has been at war for five years now. Naturally people are poorer there than they ever were before, and when that happens the number of rogues in any country increases. Plenty of people are honest in good times but cannot be in bad times because they are not made of strong enough stuff. So when you are cheated sometimes in China, as you will be, just remember that strangers are cheated in any country, and do not blame everybody for it. You will probably be asked a higher price for whatever you buy in China than you would be if you were a Chinese.

While I am on the subject of roguery in China I might mention the subject of "squeeze," which has made so many Westerners indignant in China. Yet it has long been a Chinese custom to have a certain tax taken off by persons making a transaction. Thus, a Chinese servant buying for his master will pay ten cents for oranges and charge his master eleven cents if he is loyal and as much as he can get away with if he is not. Ten percent is considered fair. Since masters and servants are both aware of the "squeeze," and since the low wages take it into account, it can scarcely be called cheating under the system as it is accepted. Its evil effects are about those of the system of tipping in our country. It would be better if neither existed and if wages could be raised.

Some things will surprise you as you go along the Chinese streets. But they need not shock you if you are ready to admit that people may be the same at heart whatever their customs. Thus you will see mothers nursing their babies on doorsteps and enjoying the life of the street while they do so. True, these may be the poorer, simpler people, but they will also be the middle-class people. Take this as a matter of course as the Chinese do and do not offend their sense of good taste by seeming even to see it. You will find everywhere in China a greater naturalism than we have in our country. The ordinary functions of life are of no moment to them and may be performed wherever nature demands. Except for nursing a child, however, this applies only to men and children. Chinese women are extraordinarily modest about themselves, generally speaking. But you will see children running about with nothing at all on, or even in winter with their trousers conveniently open, ready for emergencies. Most Chinese mothers do not much worry themselves with diapers for their children. You will also see families eating in public view in the same easygoing fashion, quarreling and working and laughing and talking with a freedom that is fascinating to watch. Life goes on very much in the open in China, far more than it does in our own country, and in many ways this makes it delightful to live in China. In fact, Chinese distrust privacy and secrecy. The same word which means *illegal* in the Chinese language means also *private* or *secret*. Why, they ask, should you try to hide something if it is not wrong?

So you will enjoy, as I have so often, walking along Chinese streets and seeing the rich human life going on around you, the ready hot-blooded quarreling, the guffaws of laughter, the dozens of children running about, the busy people arguing over their buying and selling. They will enjoy you, too. They will look at you and shout to each other. A crowd will follow you to stare at you and to discuss everything you do and how you walk and how you look. They will be a friendly crowd, you may be sure—accept them good-humoredly and let them come along. You are a good show. They will be delighted if you grin at them, and if you have a trick or two at your disposal, they will roar with laughter and be your friend forever. But of course there will be an impudent boy in the crowd who will go a step too far. When this happens, simply walk on or ignore him. Any crowd can turn from good nature into a sort of teasing if they feel a stranger is at their mercy. But your own manner can control this.

And at night before the wooden blinds are put up for the night how fascinating the Chinese streets are! The families eat their suppers by candlelight or small oil lamps —rarely is there electricity in the Chinese city—and the blacksmiths still work at their fiery forges, and shops are not yet closed. Teashops and places of amusement are going full tilt, and every scene is like a painting. If you are willing to lend yourself to China, making no comparisons with other countries, you will see a great deal of beauty in the Chinese streets. And after all, what is the use of going abroad if it is only to complain because things are not the same as they are at home?

But as you pass along the Chinese streets, especially away from the main business streets, you will often pass high walls, blank except for a single gate. These gates may be open or shut, they may be simple or very ornate with brass trimmings and stone lions. Whatever they are, they are probably well-to-do homes. The people you see so freely on Chinese streets are the plain people, the middle-class, the everyday folk. But the rich live behind the high walls.

I do not know how much opportunity will be given you to get behind those walls. I hope that you will get to know some Chinese well enough as a friend so that he will want to invite you to such a home, just that you can see what a well-to-do, cultivated Chinese home is like. If this happens, you must take it as a great compliment, for Chinese, particularly of the better-educated classes, do not easily invite strangers to their homes. Usually men meet at teahouses for talk and pleasure. Only intimate friends go to each other's houses.

But if you can enter one of those great gates, then put on your best behavior. If you see a woman, do not look at her, but go on. You will be led through a court or perhaps several courts full of flowers and shrubs to a big room which is the main room of the house. There the furniture may be very fine indeed, of polished blackwood or redwood, both valuable heavy woods, or possibly of teak from Burma.

163

Inside the backs of the chairs may be set "landscape marble" from the province of Yunnan, so-called because when it is cut across the grain it has black or dark green markings which make a scene of waves or mountains and forests. The general arrangement of furniture in such a room is always the same—a long, carved table is set against the wall facing the door as you enter. Upon this table are ornaments, a pair of candles and an urn for incense. Between the candles hangs a fine scroll or the picture of a god, or a family treasure of some sort. In front of the long table is a square table, and on either side of this an armchair. The one on the right as you enter is the seat of honor. Do not sit in this until you are pressed to do so, as you will be pressed. Then you may sit down, for after all, you are the guest. The next-important person takes the seat across the table, and the chairs on either side of small tables along the walls of the room grow less important as they approach the door. In general, what is innermost in the room or the house is the highest in importance.

What next? Your host will pour you a bowl of tea. He hands it to you with both hands, and you must take it with both hands, saying *"Hsieh-hsieh,"* or "thank you." Then you may set it down. It may have a cover on it, and if it has, use it to push aside the tea leaves, and sip from under it as you lift cup and small saucer together. Sweetmeats, if offered, should be eaten sparingly and always have a little left, to show that you have had more than you can eat. Thereafter you follow your host's lead. If he is modern and informal, you may be informal; if he is old-fashioned and rather stiff, then the quieter you are the better. You can admire generally but do not admire one object especially, for then courtesy requires your host to give it to you. Above all, in a house like this you cannot seem to see any woman. To do so would be to insult her. If there is a modern sister who is brought in and introduced, be very formal indeed and do not look at her directly when you speak—look a few inches above her head—at least until you are a very old friend and know what you are about and what the people in the house are like.

You may even be invited to a feast. It is likely the feast will not be in a home, however, but in a restaurant or hotel. If you are invited to a feast, it is still wise to eat only what is hot. You will find that the feast begins with some cold dishes. Accept what cold food is put on your plate but do not eat it. It is always perfectly good manners not to eat at a Chinese feast. Besides, there will be many hot dishes so good that you cannot keep from eating them. When the hot dishes come on, you may eat as many and much as you like. The Chinese are famous cooks, and no cooking in the world—to my mind not even French cooking—approaches theirs as an art. Moreover, Chinese are proud of their cuisine and like to talk about food, so it is perfectly good manners when you are an invited guest to ask all sorts of questions about the dishes that are new to you, how they are cooked and what they are made of. Your host will appreciate your interest.

Probably you will have chopsticks instead of a knife and fork and a bowl instead of a plate, though there will certainly be a small plate. The chopsticks must be held in one hand and are worked on the lever principle. Ask your host how to hold them—he will enjoy teaching you. Don't be surprised when he takes his own chopsticks to put food into your bowl or plate—that is a slight risk one has to take for friendship's sake. You don't need to eat the bit he puts there and you can still appreciate the fact that what he has done is good Chinese manners. If the feast is a big one, the rice will not come on until the very end with four substantial dishes of meats and vegetables to go with it or even six. The dessert will be a sweet dish and will be served in the middle of the meal. The soup will come at the very end and is supposed to wash down the meal comfortably. Afterwards there will be titbits of fruits and nuts to eat with the tea you will drink. Wine will be served with the feast in very tiny bowls. It will probably be hot wine poured from a small pewter pot. If it is Shaohsing wine, it will be of the best, though there are many grades. At any rate, you can safely drink a good many small bowls of it. But if it is Kaoliang wine, or any of the Canton wines, then be careful —they are heavy drinks.

Wine drinking is much enjoyed in China and people drink a good deal but nearly always with the meals. There is seldom any drunkenness and public drunkenness is despised. It is a sign of low breeding to be drunk in public or in fact to allow oneself to be drunk anywhere. When a Chinese feels he has drunk enough he says so, and no one presses him beyond the point. But wine they love, and they drink freely. There are many games they play while they drink, guessing games and betting games, and the loser has to drink. When your host cries, *"Kan-pei!"* it means "Bottoms up!" and you must empty your bowl with him if you can.

You may not always attend a feast. Perhaps you will go into a restaurant yourself to order a meal. It is best to go not fewer than four in number if you want a good meal. The Chinese rule, in general, is to order the number of dishes that there are persons eating, plus a soup. Rice, of course, comes with the meal. The kind of food you will get depends on where you are in China. If you are in northern China, you will get roast duck as a specialty, eaten with small pancakes and haw jelly. There will be any other meat you want and vegetables, particularly a fine white cabbage. You will get bread or millet, perhaps, instead of rice. But you can get almost anything you want.

In central and southern China you will get all sorts of fish and fowl and pork dishes, and rice generally instead of bread. Anywhere, though especially in north China and in the province of Szechuan, you will get fine noodles and breads and fried twists, like our crullers but not sweet. In Hunan you must be careful because they put red pepper in almost everything. Of course you will drink only wines and tea—milk is not a product natural to China, and if you find it even in a can it is occidental and imported. Do not drink it fresh anywhere except in homes you know. And drink no cold water unless you know it has been boiled.

What else will you see on the streets of Chinese cities? Some sights that will not please you! There will be some

wretched dogs, mangy and flea-bitten and bad-tempered—
stay away from them. They are not used to kindness or to
being touched by human beings. They are mongrels and
strays, the scavengers of the city. You will see human strays,
too, beggars of the most sorrowful sort. There will be the
professional beggars, crippled and diseased and whining.
Do not give anything to them, for if you do, you will be
besieged. They belong to a guild, just as they do in our
American cities, and what they get they give to their king,
who supports them on a minimum and guarantees that to
keep them in the gang. If you never give, they will soon
cease to trouble you, but if they once know that you may
give, your life will be made miserable.

But there will be others—refugees and homeless people,
the very poor, and now perhaps the wounded. There are
many Chinese who have suffered in this war—far more
than there have been hospitals and doctors enough to care
for. China has had this war come at a peculiarly vulnerable
time in her history. She was, before the war, only just beginning to have modern doctors and hospitals and nurses,
and public health service. War came upon her before she
could get ready for the wounded, and she has had five years
of the cruelest possible attack from land and air. The
wounded in China must now be numbered in the millions.
You will see them. What you can do to help them must be
left to you. I should say that in general it is best to give
money only privately, or at least out of public sight.

But there will be other sights that are not so tragic. Much
of the traffic on Chinese streets is increased and impeded

by the vendors who sell anything and everything—pottery, food, clothing, baskets, furniture. Each vendor has his own age-long call, and the experienced ear can hear the bean curd vendor a quarter of a mile away, or the man who sells sesame candy or peanuts or vegetable oil. One of the sounds I remember best from my own childhood in a house upon a hill in the Chinese countryside is a sweet and plaintive piping upon a short bamboo flute. It was the barley sugar man. Against the rules, if I had a penny I slipped down the hill through the shielding bamboos and paid out my coin and had in return a lump of tough barley taffy which the man chipped off with a little iron chisel and hammer from the flour-covered mass on his stand. It was always delicious and I have survived it.

And I ought to mention the freight carriers of China, the men who carry loads of anything and everything upon poles across their shoulders. Those lean, brown, tough men—they are the backbone of Chinese life. They have built the Burma Road, carrying the rocks and the soil in baskets swinging from their poles, and now that the road is lost to the enemy they are building roads again further north. Strong, indefatigable bearers of sedan chairs through city streets and up the rocky stone steps of mountainsides, carriers of goods from foreign ships into the interior of China everywhere, pushing wheelbarrows loaded with goods or human beings across cobbled country roads, pulling rickshaws—the coolies of China are among the salt of the Chinese earth. They are fighting today in guerrilla ranks, eating their scanty fare, their stomachs never filled, their bodies always nothing but bone and muscle. They are to be treated with every respect for what they are in Chinese life and in the waging of this war. When you sit behind one of them in a ricksha, consider what he is and how you can help him. He will not appreciate it if you walk instead of hiring him, for he depends upon his job to feed himself and his family. But he will appreciate your sitting forward when he goes uphill, and leaning back when he goes down, and at other times sitting with your weight in the middle of the vehicle. Pay him as well as you can, and if it is too much, remember that he is the lowest-paid man in the world for what he does.

The coolie class is a fluid one in China. One is not born into it, and if times improve one need not stay in it. It is the safety valve of unemployment, for when all other jobs are closed, one can always get a coolie job to tide him over. The word *coolie* comes from two Chinese words *ku lih,* meaning *bitter strength.*

What can you find to amuse you in Chinese cities? Some of them, though not many, have movies. The Chinese love movies, any kind of movies, as you will discover when you wedge your way into a crowded building. Do not expect comfort when you do it. The likelihood is that you will sit on an uncomfortable bench or an unstable folding chair, and that the house will be hot in summer and cold in winter. As for the picture, it may be anything. Before the war the modern cities had excellent motion picture theaters and all the new pictures almost as soon as they were released in the United States. But in the interior of China the people are not so particular. They still gaze with appreciation at the earlier efforts of Charlie Chaplin and Harold Lloyd. They love slapstick comedy and roar with laughter at the slightest touch of humor. Wild West shows they look at with pity for us and consider that the bandit problem must be very severe in America. Mae West and her sisterhood they receive with bewilderment, not sure whether to take them as the way women are in America, or as something else. But whatever the picture, they receive it with absorption and enthusiasm and a running comment freely expressed that makes half the fun of the show if you can understand it.

Very often—increasingly often now—you will see Chinese films. These films still lack a good deal in technical skill and are for the American observer curiosities rather than pictures. But to be fair it must be said that our films are that for the Chinese. The American must remember as he looks at Chinese films that frank revelation of emotion, even of fear, is allowable and sometimes admirable to the Chinese audience. There is nothing to be ashamed of, to their thinking, in a man's shedding tears publicly if he feels like it.

But it is still true that most Chinese cities do not have motion picture theaters and the places of amusement are those which the Chinese themselves enjoy. There are the theaters where Chinese plays and dramas are performed. I cannot hold out hope that the average American will enjoy these any more than the average Chinese enjoys a performance in the Metropolitan Opera House in New York. If you do try the Chinese theater it will give you a glimpse of gorgeous costumes, stereotyped action, and singing which, however it rouses the Chinese crowd to enthusiasm, will seem to you perhaps nothing but interminable wailing. I can only remind you that to the Chinese our singers seem to be screaming and caterwauling. The greatest difference perhaps between ourselves and the Chinese is in what we consider music.

In the Chinese theater the most interesting performance is not the play but what goes on around it. The property man is a figure of fun without in the least meaning to be. He comes on the stage whenever a chair has to be moved or a table adjusted. Since this is his daily job he cares nothing for the actors or the play. Blasé and solemn, he shifts scenes, proffers tea to the main actor in the midst of a great song so that he will not be exhausted, yawns, picks his ears, and stares at the crowd. The Chinese imagination is more vivid than ours and such things do not disturb them. You will see crowded on the wings of the stage, too, other persons who have obviously nothing to do with the play—men, women and children. They apparently pay no attention whatever to the performance. These are the families and friends of the actors who have free seats there.

The audience itself will bewilder you. The performance goes on for hours, and for much of the time nobody seems to look or listen to it. People eat hot food that is brought in by waiters, crack watermelon seeds between their teeth, drink pots and pots of tea, talk, play with their children, and catch the hot towels that are thrown over the heads of the crowd by expert towel throwers. These towels, wrung out of very hot water, are used to wipe the hands and faces of those who wish to be refreshed. The use of a hot towel costs —or did—in the neighborhood of a penny a time. You are advised against using them because of the prevalence of trachoma among the people.

But negligent as this crowd appears it knows when the big scenes and the famous actors are about to appear. When this moment approaches, quiet comes over them, and they become intensely attentive. If the familiar scene is well done, their approval is uproarious. Yes, the crowd is the most interesting part of the show at a Chinese theater.

Actually the Chinese shows which you may enjoy best are the little traveling theaters you will see in the country, which put on their performances in temple courts in small towns and big villages. There are Punch and Judy shows, too, in city and town, peep shows, jugglers, and contortionists. These are usually to be found on feast days and market days in the public squares that are before many of the temples.

But there may be a canal running through or near a town, or a lake. If so, certainly there will be pleasure boats to be hired, "flower boats" they are called, and for a few cents you can be poled or rowed about through shallow water studded, if it is summertime, with great rosy lotus blooms. The seeds of the lotus are as large as almond nuts and are hidden in big pods. These seeds are a delicacy which can be peeled and eaten raw when they are green, and are often used in desserts at feasts, and in candies.

Speaking of boats, perhaps this is a good point to draw your attention to the extraordinary boat life of China. Wherever there is river or lake or seacoast harbors you will find hundreds and even thousands of water craft of all kinds, from small sampans rowed with one oar to huge seagoing junks. Upon these boats live families who for generations have never lived on land. In small space or large, they bring up their children and carry on their life, earning a living by carrying goods and passengers. On the whole they have the reputation for being a gipsyish, rascally lot, but I don't know that it is justified. They trust to the water for their well-being and know no gods but the river god. Once I was on a barge floating down a dirty canal, and the boatman leaned over and dipped up a gourd full of the vile water and drank it. I exclaimed at this, saying that I would not dare to drink such stuff, and calling his attention to various unfortunate objects in the water—I remember particularly a dead puppy. To which he replied calmly, "You are very right not to drink this water—you would get sick if you did and probably die. But it won't hurt me— I make my living on this water. The old river god knows me."

Apart from these places and the teahouses where the Chinese men drink tea and talk, and the fairs and marketplaces, you will have to find your amusement in the life of the people as you see it about you. The Chinese do not have the highly organized amusement places to be found in

American cities and towns. Perhaps this is because they do not need amusement so much—they find it in the enjoyment of the everyday affairs of life.

But I have been talking mainly about cities and towns. What if you land in Chinese countryside? Well, then, you are lucky, for the Chinese country is beautiful. It is not of course beautiful in the same way that it is in America. You will notice many differences. The hills, for instance, will not often be wooded. They are usually bare and covered only with grass. The reason for this is that for long Chinese have been dependent on wood and grass for fuel. Most of the forests of China are gone, and food is now cooked in big earthen stoves with grass only. Only occasionally will there be small earthen or iron stoves for charcoal. Grass makes a quick, hot fire, and Chinese food is quickly cooked, as you will notice. There is some coal, but it is mainly in the large cities and is not very generally used, for the reason, perhaps, that mining has not been much developed in China. Indeed it may be said that China's sources in coal and ores are almost untouched and even unknown. The best of these mines are now in Japanese hands. It has thus come about that for sheer lack of any other fuel when forests were gone the people began to use grass and roots and what they could find and this has gone on for centuries. Every autumn when the grass is grown to its height and is dry the Chinese farmers and their families go out and cut their fuel in great bundles and bring it home and stack it for winter use or take it to the city to sell it. It is a beautiful sight in the clear autumn days to see the blue-coated people

175

working in the ruddy grass on the hills. At first those bare hills will seem strange and barren to you, but you will learn to like their bony outlines. Sunshine and shadow lie very sharply upon the Chinese hills.

But what that landscape is like will depend on where you land in China's eighteen provinces. It will not be the same in the north as it is in the south, and east will be different from west. China is a huge country, half again as big as the United States, and when you think of the varieties of our own country you will easily see that the variety must be as great in China, both in climate and landscape. And so it is. In the cold north you will find freezing weather very early in the autumn, and the north is flat and desertlike until you reach the mountains of the northwest. The plains of north China are flat and sandy; rice cannot be grown, and wheat and sweet potatoes, peanuts and kaoliang, a kind of soybean, are the chief crops. That sand has been blown for centuries by the bitter northwest winds from the desert of Gobi, and I suppose, in time, will spread the desert still farther, unless modern agriculture comes in to stop the process.

If you land in north China, then, you will see flat country, much like our western states of Nebraska and Kansas. There will be almost no trees except those about the earth-colored villages. The climate will be dry and dusty. In the spring there will be a season of fierce dust storms, when everything, even the people, are drab with the gray, sandy dust. Yet this sand region is beautiful in summer, when mirages lend their imaginary lakes and trees to the green fields. And the winter weather is glorious, cold and clear.

The northern people are different, too, from the southern people. They are tall—six-footers are common in north China among the men and there are plenty of tall women. Most of those women still have their feet bound, outside the cities; and men, women, and children, they will all smell of garlic and all be good-natured and jolly and somewhat dirty, for what is the use of constantly washing yourself when the wind blows dust on you again at any moment, and when water is so precious? These are the famine regions of China, for crops are uncertain because of droughts or because of floods from the Yellow River.

But if you land in central China or in western central China, you land in a fair country. There the soil is rich and the people placid with good feeding and plenty.

Houses in the arid north are of earth with straw-thatched roofs, and the towns are like desert towns, sprawling, flat-roofed, and their unpaved streets are wide. But in central and southern China the houses are of brick with tile roofs, and the streets are paved with cobbles. The people are not so tall as the northerners and they are much cleaner, for water is not scarce. There are many rivers and streams and wells, and every farm has its pond for fish and for the wallowing water buffalo, which are the labor animals. Those buffalo, by the way—carabao, they may be called—are full of race prejudice. It is better for a white man not to go near them. They look so stupid and calm, but they can be madly ferocious when they don't like you, and they don't like a white man for any reason at all. You will see them pulling the plows through watery rice fields of southern

China or through deep black soil in wheat fields of central China, but do not be misled by their placid looks.

The landscape of China, then, will vary from the dry and desertlike north through the rich central areas, lush with green fields and grassy hills and bamboo groves, to the tropical south. There is every sort of landscape in China and much of it is extremely beautiful.

But sometimes, rarely, you will see deeply wooded mountains. When you do, they will be worth climbing. They will be full of clear streams and deep pools where you can swim, and there will be gorgeous flowers and many birds, some plain-colored and sweet-singing and some gaudy in their coloring and usually stupid in their songs. Lilies of all sorts will grow on those hills, and many ferns. You will recognize some of the flowers we have in America, both wild and cultivated. In the spring there will be azaleas and we got many of our azaleas from China. In the autumn there will be chinquapins and colored oaks, though in general the Chinese autumn coloring is not so spectacular as ours. As to snakes, it is well to be careful. There are not many, as snakes go, and few are dangerous. But there is a little grass-green fellow who swings in the trees, and he is bitterly your enemy. He seldom grows more than two feet long, but he is poisonous. I have never seen a rattlesnake in China, but there are moccasins and adders.

Sometimes high on a hill or deep in a wooded valley you will come upon a temple, whose gray-robed, shaven-headed monks look at you half afraid. When you go into a Chinese temple, and you will find them in the hills and in

178

the crowded cities and in the villages, everywhere, simply behave as you would in a church in our own country. You will see the gods which the people worship. The Chinese are not a generally religious people and many of them never go near a temple. Perhaps most of the men do not. But many women believe in these gods, and the priests are the attendants of the gods. I don't think anyone believes that the great images of painted and gilded clay which you will see in the temples are in themselves gods, but they stand for gods to those who need an object before their eyes when they pray. Some temples are very large with thousands of images and some are very small. There are usually four images in the entrance building, the gods of north and south, east and west. In the next building, across the first court, there is usually a Buddha and eighteen Lohan, or subsidiary deities, corresponding to disciples. In another building there may be the Goddess of Mercy, or Kuanyin, who in Chinese Buddhism holds the same position that the Virgin Mary does in the Catholic Church. She is the special one whom women worship in China. Only Buddhist temples have these; Confucian temples have none. That is because Confucianism is not so much a religion as it is a philosophy. Confucius, who lived five hundred years before Christ, did not concern himself with man's life beyond this world. He said, "Since I cannot understand earth, how can I understand heaven, and since I cannot understand man, how can I understand God?" He busied himself, therefore, with working out the proper relationships between people and with making clear what seemed to him the essentials of

179

the superior man. Confucius has had more influence on Chinese thought and development than any other one figure.

Buddhism was a religion which grew up first in India and was imported into China by priests, just as missionaries from the West have taken Christianity into China. The Chinese resisted Buddhism for hundreds of years, and indeed accepted it only when they had made it over almost entirely and changed it from the mystical Indian Buddhism to a practical working sort of religion known as Zen Buddhism.

You will see in some temples priests not bald and shaven but wearing their hair long and knotted on top of their heads like old-fashioned women. Sometimes their robes are orange colored. These are Taoist priests, and theirs is a religion of animism, or spirits in every material object. The founder of this religion was an ancient Chinese named Lao-tse, whose sayings are still much revered. This religion appeals mostly to the simpler folk who believe in ghosts and devils more easily than other people do.

It is a symbol of Chinese tolerance and breadth of mind that a man can belong to all of these religions at the same time. It surprises the Chinese that our Western religions are exclusive, so that a man cannot be a Catholic and a Protestant, too. The practical Chinese mind reasons that if both religions are good, why not join both?

There are some Christian churches in China and these you will find mainly in cities. There used to be many Christian missionaries.

It is necessary to put in one word of caution about visiting Chinese temples. Some temples are centers for dangerous and evil characters. This has come about because priests in China have been beyond the law and temples have been sanctuary. When a man commits a crime he is safe if he becomes a priest. Therefore it is well not to go alone, especially into the more remote temples. But this is true only of a few places, and most temples are genuine places of worship and should be entered as such.

I think you will be safe in the Chinese hills, and yet in troubled times it is well to inquire whether or not bandits infest some of the mountains. Skirmishes may be as well reserved for the real enemy.

I must not forget to mention one characteristic of the Chinese countryside—the graves. The foothills and low hills of any Chinese landscape may be used as gravelands. Sometimes a family will enclose its plot with a low mud wall, and the head of the family dead will have the highest grave. In south China the coffins are set on the ground and enclosed in brick walls and a roof of tiles. This consumes a good deal of ground, and indeed the loss of acreage in gravelands in China is an agricultural problem, especially in north China, where there is no hill land and graves are set out in the fields.

You will see funerals sometimes, and can know what they are by the white-clad figures. Chinese mourning is always coarse white cotton cloth. The poor have a small funeral procession, only the family following the casket, with perhaps a white cock tied on it for sacrifice to the dead, but the rich may spend many thousands of dollars on a

181

funeral. Priests and mourners, furniture and cars and even airplanes are made of paper to be burned at the grave for the spirit's use in the future, and in sedan chairs may be the favorite objects of the one dead, and his photograph. It is best not to come too near these processions, for a stranger is not welcome at such times. Above all, do not try to take pictures.

Sometimes at the graves what you will see is not a funeral but a memorial service, when incense is burned and silver and gilt paper, too, twisted into the form of a "shoe," which used to be the unit of money exchange in the old days. Again, when this is burned it is with the idea that it will be of use to the dead. Do not be surprised if at these memorial moments you see women wailing against the grave. They are doing their duty to the dead.

But sometimes you will see unburied coffins left standing upon the ground, or see them in the vestibules or empty rooms of temples. They are waiting for a lucky burial day. Chinese believe very much in astrology, and all the important events of their lives are arranged by geomancers who study the stars and the numbers to discover the right days. You will see these geomancers in almost any town and city —usually little old men with large spectacles and scanty beards, sitting behind a table spread over with a grayish white or blue cloth, on which are many little paper-bound books. The geomancers, to eke out a living, will also write letters for those who cannot write.

Death is perhaps not quite so final in China as it is with us. The dead one is still a member of the family. His name is in the family hall, carved on a tablet, among the tablets of the oldest dead, and at certain times of the year all are especially remembered. For three generations after one is dead he is still considered to be an active member of the family. After that he is considered to be dissolved into pure spirit. The constant remembrance of ancestors has made for family and national solidarity in China, and has given a sort of immortality to the individual.

What of the people who live in the Chinese countryside? You will see at once that they do not look like city people. There is the same difference between the way the country and city people look in China as there is in America— probably more, for China has no mail-order houses. That is, country people wear older clothes and more old-fashioned ones than city people do. Farmers usually wear blue trousers and coat for everyday work wear, and when it is hot nothing but the trousers rolled to the knee. They go barefoot or wear straw sandals or homemade cotton socks and cloth shoes. Women wear trousers and jacket and when they dress they put on a pleated black silk skirt. In the north they wear black kerchiefs over their hair, but in the south go bare-headed except in winter, when they put on a ban- deaulike hat that has no crown.

City people, men and women, usually wear robes unless they are working people, and the styles change as often as they do in American cities. The Chinese modern dress for women is very pretty indeed—a long, close-fitting robe with or without a collar, and with long or short sleeves. On the slender Chinese figure it is extremely smart and graceful. City people, men and women, have their hair short these days, although older women often have long hair still, and since Madame Chiang has never cut her hair, she has set a style for some of the younger women, too. Country girls seldom cut their hair, and though the men nearly always have short hair, in remote parts of China one can still see an occasional queue. Foot binding has disappeared from cities in all except the older generation of women, but is still seen sometimes in the country, especially in north China. It seems an astounding custom to the Westerner, but the Chinese like to retort that it was never as bad in its effects as lacing used to be a generation ago in our country. Perhaps they are right.

You will be surprised perhaps to see that nearly all country people live in villages. It is very seldom that one sees an isolated farmhouse in China. Farmers go out to farm their fields but at night they come home to the village. These villages are very near to each other, perhaps as far away from each other as the average farmhouses in this state of Pennsylvania in one of which I am at this moment writing. They are usually within sight and walking distance of one another.

Yet each village is its own little unit. Very often all of its people are related by blood, near or distant, and the only strangers are the women who come from some other village to be married. Chinese are very careful not to marry inside the family group. It is a general rule that one may not marry a person of the same surname.

Sometimes the village has a low wall of mud or brick

about it, if it is large enough to seem a small town, but usually there is no wall. A walled village is usually a market town, which corresponds to the small town in America. The village proper may have only one street, or it may have more. Usually it has only one business street, and here you will find a simple inn, its unpainted tables under an awning of patched blue cloth. You can get a good bowl of noodles and soup here if you are hungry and plenty of tea. If you are willing to wait, the innkeeper or his wife will make you some scrambled eggs to eat with a bowl of rice, and a dish of green cabbage and bean curd, or a brown fish. The bean curd you will not like at first but try it until you do—it has valuable protein qualities, and is the poor man's meat. Rice and green cabbage and bean curd are what keep the Chinese farmer healthy and industrious and full of Chinese pep.

There will be besides the inn a small shop, like a general store in an American village, selling a little of everything, and then the farmers' houses, of earth or brick and often straw-thatched, straggle along the rest of the streets.

The country people will be shy and inclined to be afraid when they see you. I have traveled in parts of China where white persons were unknown and when we approached a village the entire population took to the fields, and would not come back until we went away again. But this is not usual. You will find farmers and their families, as in our own country, shy of strangers, not quite ready to smile until they are sure of you, and yet kind and hearty and friendly when they know you mean well. They are, like all

Chinese, full of laughter and hearty good humor, and it is a pity not to be able to understand their language for it is so full of earthy jokes, of good puns, and sharp observations.

The Chinese are fine farmers, and you will see carefully cultivated fields, small by our standards, but highly productive, and their vegetable gardens put ours to shame. At the same time do not be surprised, especially in the central and southern parts, if you smell an unholy foulness over the most beautiful gardens. This comes from the night soil that is used as fertilizer. It is kept in large earthen jars sunk in the ground and water is poured over it. It is allowed to soak until it is rotted and then it is spread over the growing crops with a long-handled dipper out of two wooden buckets slung on a pole in which the farmer carries it to the garden. That the crops appreciate it is all too evident, but it is another reason why no vegetables must be eaten raw in China.

The Chinese farmhouse is very simple indeed. What you will see of it is, first, a low earthen-walled house with a thatched roof, one or two small windows or none, and outside the door a threshing floor. This is the poor farmer's house. There are many others far better, the walls of brick and the roofs of tile, and inside the gate there may even be several courts and many rooms. Sometimes there is a low tower. It is a watch tower and is used to guard the crops against thieves, fire, and bandits.

The architecture of Chinese houses everywhere in city and country has a similarity which is the result of long living in one spot of the globe by the same kind of people.

186

The variety in our American architecture is due perhaps to the variety in the people who came to make our country, people from many lands and many races. But China has developed her own style of building. Thus anywhere in China you will find houses built about a court, if they are large enough, and this whether they are the houses of rich or poor, of farmer or official. The roof lines, too, though generally simple and straight in dwelling houses, follow upsweeping curves in temples and public buildings. In northern architecture these lines are long and gentle, following, perhaps, the flattened lines of a countryside without hills. But in south China, where there are many sharply rising hills, the roof lines sweep abruptly up, and there may be many little ornaments of animals and bells.

Anywhere in China you may see towers in stories. These are pagodas, and the idea of them came originally from India. In the north they appear in the shortened and less graceful form called dagobas. A pagoda is set at an important point in the landscape and usually has an astrological purpose and is often connected with a temple. I remember a very beautiful pagoda that stood on an island in the Yangtze River near the place where I spent my childhood. That pagoda, I was told and long believed when I was small, was built there to hold down the head of an immense subterranean dragon. If he were not thus imprisoned, he would roil and ruin the river and wreck the countryside about.

There is exactly the same relationship between farmer and city man in China that there is in any other country: mutual distrust and mutual scorn of each other's ways and looks. But in China the farmer, nevertheless, has a very high position in the social scale and so he should have, since about eighty-five percent of China's population of four hundred and fifty million people is rural.

It is natural that you should be interested in the Chinese army. The position of the soldier in China has undergone a great change in the last generation. He is now an honored and essential part of new China because of his splendid heroic part in this war. But in the old days his was considered the lowest of all professions. "Good iron is not made into nails or good men made into soldiers" is an old Chinese proverb. The Chinese have always believed that war is an evil and destructive thing and they tried to isolate from society, as far as possible, all those temperaments that love to make war for its own sake. This they were able to do for centuries because China was the strongest power in Asia, and without military conquest the countries around her sent tribute to the Chinese emperor. Even when China was attacked by such fierce and war-loving peoples as the Mongols and Manchus, and in a military sense conquered, she always in the end conquered her victors by her superior civilization.

For time has never meant anything in China. In four thousand years of continued life upon the same soil, each generation looks upon itself as the link between past and future. If one generation suffers, they are able to endure it and live out their time, working not for themselves but for the ones to come. Thus, more than once, China, merely by continuing to be herself, to speak her own language and keep her own culture, subdued the less civilized militarists who had conquered her, and did this without force.

Yet there were warlords in China, too. Men with the natural disposition to be soldiers were born in China, as they are in any country.

Such persons gathered around them kindred spirits and made robber gangs or local armies. Battles were fought between rival groups, but these wars seldom spread over a large territory, and did not involve outer countries. Government-maintained armies continually tried to act as police to control these gangs and succeeded only partly. A good deal of hero-worship gathered about some of these bandit gangs, because oftentimes the leaders were heroic figures, Robin Hoods who robbed only the rich and helped the poor. One of the great novels of China, *Shui Hu Chuan* (*All Men Are Brothers*), was written about such a robber band. Another great novel, *The Three Kingdoms,* was written about a period in history when China was divided into three parts and war was waged between their civil leaders. Both of these novels are in English translation. In them you will find in story form the military tactics of ancient China, the same tactics which Chinese soldiers use today so successfully, especially in guerrilla warfare. It surprised and interested me as I was reading the novels to discover that more than a thousand years ago Chinese soldiers made very good bombs much like the small bombs used today in the West. There were cannons, too, which even fired with powder, and rocks shot out of great catapults.

But the soldier did not come into his own until modern

times, when Sun Yat-sen, in the revolution to which he devoted his life, gathered together young men and made them into a revolutionary party. Yet even Sun Yat-sen, whom the modern Chinese think of as their George Washington, was not able to build a modern army. That remained to be done finally by Generalissimo Chiang Kai-shek.

Today Chinese fighting forces may be roughly divided into two parts, the national army and the guerrillas. The guerrillas have had a noble part in the war against Japan, for they have been able to function where the regular army could not. They have been made up of all kinds of people, men who were farmers by day and soldiers by night, students, and women and young men who were the middle working class in normal times. In this war the guerrillas have kept up a continual harassment of the enemy, attacking garrisons and outposts, destroying communications and food stores, killing Japanese wherever they were found alone or in small groups, using weapons and poison and any means they had. They have been zealous and desperate, caring nothing for their own lives, and living off of such food as they could find, unpaid and half starving often, their weapons mainly what they could seize from the enemy. Such bands soon learn camouflage and ambush and secret attack. They can march and merge into the landscape so thoroughly that they can scarcely be seen. The country people protect and shield them, and when the enemy comes out to fight them they are not to be found. Yet as soon as the enemy's back is turned, they are there again.

The regular national army numbers some four and a

half million men. They are well trained and formidable soldiers, though only moderately well armed even in small weapons. The Chinese army has little heavy artillery and no planes except the few that have been imported from the United States. China did not prepare for this war. She had a great deal to do after the overthrow of the old imperial government in 1911. A period of confusion followed that overthrow, much like our own period of confusion after our own Revolutionary War, and it was not until 1927 that a firm new government was established in Nanking, mainly by the efforts of Generalissimo Chiang Kai-shek. But China is so vast, so many reforms were needed at once, that, with her ancient aversion to militarism, national funds were put into improved roads, a modern school system, hospitals and factories and banks. A great military academy was established at Whampoa, near Canton, however, and from that academy have come most of China's best officers. In addition to the academy China has had foreign military advisors, mainly from Germany until this war broke out, and the Generalissimo has tried to modernize the army as quickly as possible amid all else that had to be done under a form of government totally new to China. Chinese, as you know, make fine soldier material, and the people have come to honor the soldiers very much in this war.

The democratic form of government which China chose after her revolution was based on the government of the United States with certain changes. So far there has been allowed only one party, the Kuomingtang, or national party. But other parties are already developing. After the war is over there will undoubtedly be a second party in the Communist group who have fought so well as guerrillas all during the war. The Communists in China are not to be confused with the Bolshevist type. China is too large a country to take wholesale anything from another country. The Chinese Communists are not so much Communists in the early Russian sense as they are agrarian reformers, who believe in bettering the life of the rural population, some of whom suffer much from absentee landlordism, outrageously high taxes, and usury. The Chinese farmer has as yet little security.

It is doubtful, though, that China could have progressed so quickly in her new government had the people not been long accustomed to a practical democracy. They were used to governing themselves because actual government in China has for centuries been centered in the family system. Thus even under the empire, the emperor was only the titular and spiritual head of the government, and he had a viceroy in every province who represented him but did not have the power of life and death. When a crime was committed the criminal was always sent back to his home town and judged by his fellows, even to the death sentence.

Another strong democratic force in old China was the examinations to which anybody was eligible. These were examinations in literature and philosophy and history, and whoever passed in the highest class were the ones from whom the officials were chosen. The bright son of a farmer would be as likely to pass as the son of a scholar or rich man, and thus many of China's great men came from humble families. The Chinese have the same log cabin tradition that we do, only they call it "the grass hut."

Another democratic practice of old China was that no son could inherit a title. When Lord Macartney, the head of the first British mission to the Chinese emperor, presented his nation's gifts to the throne, there was among them a book of photographs of the English peerage. The Chinese were very much shocked because there was a little duke of six years in the book. "It is impossible that a child could deserve to be a duke," they said.

These and other democratic habits have made of the Chinese a people democratic to the core, used to governing themselves and managing their own lives. You will notice how well they carry themselves and how independent they seem, even the servants and the men who pull rickshas. And they are independent for they are free men and have always been free men. A servingman in China will serve you well and shrink from nothing in the course of his duty. But if you treat him as less than a human being he will not serve you, or if he needs the money too badly to quit the job, he will despise you. Perhaps white men lower themselves in Chinese esteem more often by the way they behave to servants than in any other way. The Chinese are used to servants—every family except the very poor has them. But they are treated with respect. They have their place and they keep it, but they are never to be held as inferiors. A trusted Chinese servant is treated like a member of the family although he would never sit at the table with the family and would be disturbed if he were asked to do so.

But he is always spoken to courteously and thanked for his services.

All this means that China is a true democracy even if her forms of democratic government are not exactly like our own. There is no reason why they should be the same so long as the democratic spirit remains strong in individuals.

Certainly democracy and the freedom of the individual in China are the reasons why the Chinese have fought so bravely in this war. As I said, when Japan attacked China the Chinese were far from ready. Generalissimo Chiang had seen the attack coming, as had many others, and he played desperately for time. But the moment came when the people demanded resistance, and ready or not, China plunged into war. Five million people it is estimated have been lost. Fifty millions have been thrown out of their homes. But the Chinese have not wavered in their resistance nor will they waver. They are deserving of every aid we can give them.

And now what more shall I say to you as you set your faces toward China? I am an American and I love my own country better than any other. But if I were not an American, I should choose to be a Chinese, because of the greatness of the Chinese people.

Yes, and because in spite of some physical discomforts I think people have a happier time in China than they do in most countries because they are treated as individuals from the moment they are conceived until a hundred years after they are dead. A person's life there starts not from birth but from conception, so that when you are born you are a year old already. All through your life you are treated with consideration as a human being. You may not have enough to eat, but you will not have your feelings hurt if it can be helped. And as you grow older you will be treated with increasing respect. The Chinese honor their old for their wisdom. It is the best country in the world for the old. They are not cast aside as they too often are in our country and considered a burden and useless. In a Chinese family the oldest member is the head and the others defer to him. At the same time, he relinquishes active work long before our elders do. As soon after forty as a Chinese can retire he does so, letting his sons take his place. But retirement does not mean any lessening in his worth to his family and to society, but an increase. Now he has time to think and to consider and to use the weight of his advice where it is most needed. In China a man or woman is not measured by what active work he does but by the quality of his personality. It is the country where individualism today is most thoroughly practiced and most highly respected.

In spite of this individualism China has fought a more unified war against the enemy than any other nation. It is well to remember this now when too many people are telling us that we must give up our individualism to achieve unity. China's individuals have given up nothing—they have simply united on the one determination to drive out the enemy and win the war.

How shall you behave in China? Certainly, above all else, you must meet them on terms of perfect equality, for Chinese are trying very hard now to meet Americans on terms of equality. It is not easy for them always, because for centuries they have considered themselves our superiors. It has been a hard struggle for the Chinese to realize that a people as young as Americans, of such mixed origins, such mingled cultures, could be their equals and, of course, the Chinese have never thought the white race superior to others. They do not believe in the superiority of any race over another.

You will realize that the one thing they will not tolerate from you, therefore, is any action which smacks of superiority merely because you are white or American. If you are a superior person, they will recognize it. But do not assume superiority because you were born a particular color or nationality.

One reason why the Chinese will not tolerate race superiority is that the experience of the Chinese with the white people has not always been fortunate. I remember a certain club in Shanghai which used to allow none but white people to enter its doors. The great Li Hung-chang, who had been a guest in the White House in Washington and at Court in London, had to come in this club in Shanghai by the service entrance if he were invited there as a guest. This sort of thing does not do for allies today.

Taking for granted, then, that you will meet Chinese on terms of basic equality, beyond that you can behave as you would among strangers in America, among people whom you do not know or have just met, upon whom you would like to make a good impression. This will not be hard, for Americans and Chinese are very much alike in

196

temperament. I think it is partly because we both live in wide countries where there is plenty of space. We are not cramped peoples. We have variety of climate and food and landscape. All this affects peoples more than we know. Certainly the similarities of China and America have produced two peoples amazingly alike and congenial, in spite of difference in race and history. China is so homogeneous in race, so ancient and united in history, and we so varied in our races and so new in our history. But because we are alike, Chinese and Americans, this means that you will very soon feel at home in China. You can feel at home as soon as you forget such surface and unimportant things as the difference in costume and food and furniture. What matters is the way people feel and think and enjoy, and in these important things the Chinese are like us.

But if I should mention a few *don'ts* for China, they would be these:

Don't put your hands on anybody, in fun or fury or affection, until you know the person very well indeed. The Chinese dislike casual personal contact. Only the modern ones like even to shake hands, and many of them secretly prefer not to do so.

Don't lose your temper for anything if you want to keep the respect of the Chinese. You will see plenty of Chinese lose theirs, but they are looked upon and look on themselves as lower class when they do so.

Don't touch goods you do not intend to buy in a shop.

Don't step across the handles of a ricksha or the bearing

pole of a chair carrier or a man with a burden—he will say nothing but will look at you mournfully, because it will bring him, he thinks, bad business for a year.

Do not be shocked if no one helps a man or woman in danger of death from some accident. Such a person is looked upon as having met his destined fate, either as punishment or from some wish of Heaven. The one who saves such a person must take responsibility for the life saved.

Don't try to take pictures unless you are very sure of your crowd. In many parts of China there is a superstition that a photograph magically removes a person's soul. Friends may be charmed to have their pictures taken, but a crowd may turn ugly at the sight of a camera.

If a mother shields her child with her hand or her apron as you go by, don't be offended. There is a saying that foreigners sometimes cast an evil shadow. Smile and let it pass. When they know you they will know that your shadow is not evil. Simply to say, "I am an American," often removes the curse.

Beyond these few precautions and a few others that you will learn either through the kindness of your Chinese friends or from force and necessity, simply be American, in the best sense. The Chinese don't expect you to be Chinese or to know all their ways of polite behavior. They will not think the less of you if you break a rule or two if they are convinced of your wish to respect them and to be friendly with them.

I have only one more thing to say as you sail for China. You go in a sense as the first ambassador of the American people to the Chinese people in our new relationship as allies. Chinese have seen a few devoted and high-minded and sometimes queer American missionaries. They have seen a few American businessmen. But most of the people of China have never seen an American of any kind. They have heard good things of America—that we have sent them relief in time of famines in the past, that we have kept other nations from dividing up the territory of China when she was too weak to resist. They look on us as their friends and they know we are now their allies. But what we are like they do not know. To the Chinese people you stand for America—you will stand for all of us here at home. It depends on you whether China will like us or not, and trust us or not.

And trust us she must, and like us she must, because we need China as much as she needs us right now, and perhaps in the future we are going to need China even more than she needs us. China is going to sit at the peace table with us after this war is won, and at that table we need a country or two that likes us and trusts us and believes in the kind of people Americans are. More than that, we need Chinese wisdom at the peace table, and Chinese sense of justice, Chinese tolerance and understanding. It is much more likely that we shall have a lasting peace after this war if Chinese help us to make it, for they are more experienced in human relations than any people now on earth. When you go to China to help win the war, therefore, you go not only to win the war but to win the peace. Remember who you are—you're America.

12

Where the Chinese People Stand

O<small>F ALL THE PEOPLES</small> of the world at this moment perhaps the most voiceless are the people of China. This is not because they are naturally inarticulate but because there is no channel now through which they can speak to other peoples. Even in wartime the French have the Free French, Russia has her spokesmen everywhere, the peoples of England and the United States speak as they will.

But the voice of the Chinese people cannot be heard. They have their official representatives abroad, but the Chinese people feel that these are not saying all the things they themselves want said. The resolute, resurgent voice of the people which was so clear before the fall of Hankow is muted. What has become of the Chinese people? How much of the silence is simply the silence necessary because of censorship and difficulties of war? It is time to answer these questions not only for the sake of the Chinese

Written in 1943.

200

people but also for the sake of the American people who are their friends.

I say this because American friendship for China has now reached a popular height which brings it to the verge of sentimentality. The Chinese are being exalted into persons such as cannot exist in our fallible human race. The danger is that in our adoration we allow ourselves to come to an extreme that is dangerous to our mutual welfare because it will inevitably end in disillusionment, a disillusionment which will be unjust to the Chinese and harmful to us.

It is of course natural that the American people should, by our friendliness, wish to compensate somewhat for the practical inadequacies of our behavior toward the Chinese. We have a sense of guilt, inevitable after the knowledge, spread so widely, that certain Americans continued to sell war materials to Japan for use in China. That sense of guilt has been deepened by our other failures—the failure to insist that the Burma Road be kept open, the failure to insist that China be treated as an ally equal to England and Russia, the failure to send adequate war materials to China. Now all these failures are being merged into one vast sense of guilt as we realize, and accept, perforce, the fact that China is being relegated to a third-rate place both in the war and in the peace. Our genuine fondness of the Chinese, combined with our sense of guilt, is making us rush to pour out the warmth of our hearts where we cannot exercise the judgment of our minds. Money for relief, personal gifts from Americans to Chinese, and extravagant praise are the ways in which we are trying to compensate to China.

A dose of common sense is now needed. If the dose is not taken in time, those who have rushed to give the gifts, those who have sold valued possessions, as some have, to make a gift, are going to wake up one morning to condemn China and all Chinese, and then they will regret their possessions and feel ashamed of their emotionalism. The Chinese people deserve neither the adoration nor the condemnation. It is time to view the Chinese neither as angels nor devils but as ordinary human beings, struggling along with the rest of us to make the best of a strange world.

Where do the Chinese people stand today? For the Chinese people are still China. However bewildered they are, and they are bewildered, however stalemated and confused, the people are still China, and we must not forget that. All future plans for China, if they are sensible, practical plans, must be based on the fact that the ultimate power, if for the time being only the power of revolt, lies with the people. They may be a long time making up their minds to use it, but they will use it if they are driven to it.

If I were to mark the exact place at which the Chinese people stand today, I should have to put up a sign of the crossroads. They are at a crossroads—the crossroads between something which might be a sort of new empire, and democracy. Why not say openly what everybody who knows China knows? Why not tell the American people what the Chinese people want them to know? The Chinese people are eager that we in America should recognize their situation, because they want a genuine cooperation between our two peoples in the future, and how can this cooperation be genuine if it is built on the false suppositions of sentimentality and diplomacy? Here then is the truth as the Chinese people see it. The truth has to do with the past, with the present, and with the future.

The war in China started as a people's war. The government was reluctant to begin it, knowing that China was ill prepared for any war. The people knew that, too, and yet they saw that the war had come upon them whether they were ready or not, and that there were only two alternatives —either they had to fight with whatever they had, or they had to surrender to Japan without fighting. They chose as Americans would have chosen—as any independent, self-respecting people would have chosen—they chose to fight. It is the people of China whom we must thank today for the years of resistance against Japan. Those intrepid, reckless, plain people did for us in Asia what England did in the West—they proved the enemy was not invincible. All over China the plain people were roused—they were fighting for Chinese soil, as the Russian people are fighting for theirs today.

This continued until after the fall of Hankow. Then by subtle, to this day only half-understood, forces, the war slipped out of their hands. Ask an ordinary Chinese citizen today what happened and he will not be able to explain it to you. He will say, looking very puzzled, "Who knows how? We only know that before Hankow every one of us felt that the war was his war. We organized ourselves in any way we could and fought the Japanese wherever we saw them. Then we heard that this was not a good way to fight. We heard that the Jap devils could be beaten only by regular armies, by weapons from America and by the newest and most expensive foreign planes, of which we had none. We were somehow made to understand that we must wait for these things, and that the government must take the lead."

"Who told you so?" I asked one such man.

"That was the strange thing," he said. "Nobody knew where the orders came from—it was talk from mouth to ear by the time it got to us."

"So you stopped fighting?" I asked.

"Certainly not," he said, "we kept on, but you see it became complicated—one was suspected of being Communist when one fought as one had before—that is, anywhere, anyhow. So the heart was divided between fear of the enemy and fear of the hand on the shoulder."

After the fall of Hankow, it is agreed by all, the war ceased to be the people's war against Japan. It became a much more organized affair, whose responsibility lay with the officials, "Those Above" as the Chinese so eloquently call them, and the people's efforts were not welcomed.

There were of course reasons for this. It is now common knowledge among Americans, or it ought to be, that all is not well with Chinese internal affairs. Certain undemocratic forces which could not do their work so long as China was hopeful of her place as an equal ally of the United States and England have been strengthened by the policy which first relegated Japan to the place of a secondary enemy and then allowed Burma to be lost. In the isolation and helplessness of China those in the government who were voices for the people and for democracy could not speak loudly and clearly as once they did. Division within China is deepening. Without laying the blame on anybody for this, it is well to consider some facts again, present facts which have their roots in the past.

The revolution begun by Sun Yat-sen has always been divided between the right wing and the left wing. The division began with Sun Yat-sen himself. Those who know the story of his life will remember that he visited many countries seeking help in overthrowing the old Manchu empire, and nowhere found any help until he came to Russia. For this no one can be blamed. It was hardly likely that the responsible, settled governments of such countries as the United States and Britain could look with anything like respect on a wildcat young man of no particular standing who came out of China, an established empire for centuries, with the idea of overthrowing that empire and turning it into a republic. Only Russians lent him an ear and so, somewhat against his will, for he knew there were certain fundamental differences between his people and the Russians, Sun Yat-sen accepted what help he could get and went back to China.

After many failures, he succeeded in the mad dream of overthrowing the empire. Had he been as able to establish the republic as he was to overthrow the empire, China would have had better luck. But it is seldom the same man who can overthrow and build up again, and Sun Yat-sen's attempts to build were failures. He finally embodied his ideas in a sort of testament, entitled *The Three Principles of the People*. It is this testament which the Chinese have been trying to put into practice ever since.

Alas, the testament itself is divided. The first two-thirds of it are pro-Marxist enough to provide ample food for those who believe to this day that Sun Yat-sen favored the Marxist method of approach to the people's problems. But the last third presents a swing back to the right. The reason for this is well known. Between the interval of the first two-thirds and the last third of his testament, Sun Yat-sen happened upon a book written by an unknown American, Maurice Williams. This book was against Marxism, and presented the idea that true socialism had a sounder method. Sun Yat-sen was certainly influenced by the book, for he quotes from it at length, and the change in his views gave room for those who to this day believe that he was anti-Marxist.

This fundamental division in their leader's thinking has resulted in endless division among his followers. Before 1927 the revolutionary party was leftist and under the direct influence of Bolshevism. Then a young military man, a personal disciple of Sun's, rose rapidly to first place. Leading the revolutionary armies down the Yangtze valley, ever with violence but always with victory, he hastened ahead of his armies before they reached the ancient capital of Nanking, and went to Shanghai. There strong forces played upon him. One of these forces was the power of established business, both Chinese and foreign. The second force was that of the rich family with whom Sun Yat-sen had earlier allied himself through his wife, Soong Ch'ing-ling.

It could scarcely be expected that a young man of an ambitious temperament could resist these two forces. Indeed, there are many who felt he did well to cooperate with instead of resisting them, and who can say they are wrong? Had the new China developed under the leftist influence, she would today be a different country, and it is not easy to say exactly what she would have been.

Armed then with money and with influence, the young general, whose name was Chiang Kai-shek, abruptly turned the tide of the revolution from the left to the right. In this he was aided again by circumstances. The leftist army had behaved with such excesses in the old city of Nanking, in what is now known as the Nanking Incident, that all foreign powers were outraged and ready to give aid to any Chinese government which promised stability and order. This government the general set up with amazing speed.

Such speed could only be at the cost of an equally amazing ruthlessness. In those days a purge of leftist persons, and of all those even accused of leftism, was carried on with a severity, a silence that was terrifying to those who knew another China. The purge fell heaviest upon the young, who had been naturally the most revolutionary. All leftists were to be eliminated. If most of them were obscure, rather pitiable little students carried away by the tide of the times, many of them were the brilliant and the strong, and China lost when they were killed. By such means the rightists established themselves.

The people on the whole remained stupefied throughout. It was not that they did not understand what was going on —it was rather that they understood too well, and approved of neither the right nor the left. Communism in the Bolshevist sense is repugnant to the Chinese people. The principle of Communism on a national scale seems absurdly impractical to them. They believe in private property and are bourgeois in their attitude toward life. They are, moreover, realistic toward official morals, and cannot believe that officials will carry on such a scheme as Communism without private profit. In those days, I remember, the common people made no bones about their longing for the old kind of government where officials were few and one knew who the oppressors were. "Under this republican form of government," they used to remark frequently and loudly, "we never know what little turnip will cry out that he is an official and come to collect taxes. We used to have to fatten only one county magistrate—now there is the head of this bureau and the head of that, and each thinks himself the magistrate." However, the people remained prudent and calm even during the purge, in spite of great personal grief over the dead. Let the new government prove itself, they said.

But the division continued. The beaten leftists retired into country districts and began to gather strength among the peasants of certain regions, notably those, not actually many, where absentee landlordism flourished. They were relentlessly pursued by the rightists wherever they were. At length, so desperate did they become that they left en masse the regions within the power of the rightists and retired by that remarkable trek known as the Long March into the northwest, where they have been centered ever since.

By this means China came to have a semblance and to some extent even a reality of unity. The Chinese people, spectators still in all the fray, settled down. Cruelty there had been on both sides and ruthlessness, as well. The leftists often committed barbarities upon villages and peasants who did not wish to join them. In their way, they too were absolutists and the Chinese people would like to have been freed of them all, right and left together. This being impossible, they took up life as they found it, accepted the forcible devastation of their old cities such as Nanking, in order to make it possible to build new ones more like Chicago and San Francisco, and tried as ever to make a living.

The government then entered upon what was called, after Sun Yat-sen's directions, the period of reconstruction, or "People's Tutelage." There was no such thing yet as a formal or organized democracy. Perhaps there could not be. Most of the people were illiterate and a modern ballot system was impossible. The imagination of the rightists was not sufficiently strong to encourage them to devise other forms of the popular ballot more suitable to the Chinese plain man, who, though often illiterate, was neither uninformed nor unthinking. He was, as a matter of fact, accustomed to self-government, for the real government of the people for centuries had been mainly in villages and by local groups. But imbued with Western ideas, and indeed the government was made up largely of degree men from American and European universities, the rightists felt democracy must wait on literacy.

It is to their credit that they established almost overnight a system of new public schools, modeled on those of America, but even more complete, at least in plan, ranging from the kindergarten to the end of university life, all coeducational. But this is only one of their accomplishments which were very real. A new code of laws was made, new railroads built, new automobile roads, new industries established. If these were not widespread, they were amazingly so when the whole expanse of China is considered.

The great fault in the whole government scheme was, however, that it did not grow out of the people and had no roots in the native genius of the people. Young Chinese men and women who had grown up abroad and mainly in America, the product of American schools and American ways of life, undertook out of their foreign experience to make a new life for the Chinese people who had been living a deeply satisfying life of their own for centuries. True, the old life was not so hygienic as it might have been, the surfaces were not always clean in village and city, but it was human and comfortable, and the modern techniques could have been skillfully grafted on to the old roots without pain. The Chinese people are reasonable and open-minded and not averse to change when it is not imposed upon them violently. But change was imposed violently by sudden laws, enforced by rough young gendarmerie and police, and there was much pain and less result than there ought to have been.

Not only were the young rulers foreign in their thinking and experience, but when they came back to China after they had received their foreign degrees, they did not mend their ignorance of their own people. Instead of going out into the provinces and finding out what China was like and what their own people were, it is the gravest indictment against them that they remained almost always in such cities as Shanghai and Tientsin and Hankow, congregating together in a sort of Newport society of their own, reading Chinese poetry, it is true, but the old esoteric poetry and the dying classics, and repeating the painted emotions of the T'angs. These echoes of the past they wove into the new techniques they had brought back from abroad and they thought they were the new China.

However much they might have been a facet of the new China, the real China went on far beyond their comprehension. The plain people of China, neither rightists nor leftists, were pursuing their even paths, going to the new schools, riding on the new roads, but living their own way and thinking their own thoughts. They called their officials the "college boys and girls," and obeyed them good-humoredly when necessary, but did not take them too seriously. Time, teaches all, they used to say—"give them time."

At this point the Japanese attacked. The past was ended and the present began. New China, the plain people, rose to the attack.

Under this attack it became necessary to have real leaders and the people knew it. Of all those who had been leading them, Chiang Kai-shek now remained the figure they understood best. He was a true Chinese and he was a soldier and they needed a leader who understood military affairs. Left and right alike, the people united under him. They understood very well that there were forces connected with him and playing upon him that were not good forces from the point of view of the people, but in their need they had to accept the evil with the good. Moreover, they were convinced that Chiang was still stronger than these forces. They knew him to be an unsentimental man at heart, and a man who would not, therefore, allow personal emotions to sway him too deeply. They believed that he had passed the stage, too, of personal greed. He had wealth and power sufficient for him and the need for these things was not a disease with him as it is with some.

Around the figure of Chiang Kai-shek, then, the people centered. He became the symbol of their unity, and so he has continued to this day, even though the war has ceased to be a people's war. The people still hope and believe that when the clouds are cleared away from the point where they now stand, that Chiang's figure, at least, will still be there, ready for the future. Even the leftists, now once again bitterly repressed and ignored, believe that it is still possible to find unity in Chiang Kai-shek.

Are they right or wrong? Who can tell? The complexities of the present in China are very severe. Never were a people more reluctant than the Chinese people are now to consider revolution or civil war, even in the future. There can be none during the war, of course. The repression is too severe for that even if there were the will for it. The old accusations of Communism are strong enough again to make a young student disappear from a school, to close the waters of a river over a head. But even for the future the Chinese people are weary of war and struggle. "We do not want a civil war"—I have heard the words repeated again and again from young Chinese and old, from hopeless Chinese and from hopeful ones. Nobody in China wants a civil war ever again if it can be avoided.

And yet, all the people are agreed that certain evils now existing must go and certain goods must be established. The chief evil that must go is official corruption, first in high places but everywhere as quickly as possible. The only way to get rid of this corruption is by putting the power into the hands of the people. The people must be able to accuse and dismiss their officials where corruption is proved.

But this means that they must also be able to choose their rulers and this means that the technique of a democracy must be put into their hands. They had the technique of the old forms very well in their hands. Even during the days of empire the plain people of China governed themselves in matters pertaining to their everyday lives. There were certain oppressions, of course, as when labor was conscripted for imperial use. But such conscriptions were not constant. Today the old techniques are useless and new ones have not been given them. The people have no way of choosing their rulers, no way of indicting them when they are corrupt, no way of dismissing them from public office. The people of China now can only endure whatever corrupt officials choose to inflict upon them. The personal efforts of the Generalissimo are not enough to counteract this widespread and deep-seated evil, and this not only because it is too widespread but also because it is in places so high, so close to him.

This the people very well know. They do not blame him, but they hope that he can free himself. They still feel he is a great man but his greatness for the future depends upon how strong he can be in dealing with these evils on the negative side, and in providing them with a technique of democracy on the positive side.

In this state of mutual uncertainty it is inevitable that certain forces of evil are for the moment strengthening themselves, as they tend to do in similar periods in the history of any country. There is now no freedom of the press in China, nor freedom of speech. Repression is severe upon all citizens, and the implement of repression is through an organization far more severe than the secret service of a democracy ought to be. Insecurity of individuals in power breeds repression upon the people.

Recognizing the situation fully, what do the Chinese people ask for the future? They ask above all that the American people remember that they believe in democracy, and that they earnestly long for and will work for a democratic government in all ways that they can. They ask that when the American government makes its great loans for reconstruction in China, it will make them somehow to the people, to be used by the people, for the people, and not to establish any group, either right or left, by undue favor. "It is we who must return the loans," they say, "and it is to us the loans should be made." They recognize the difficulty of this, both now and in the future, but they rely on the genuine friendliness of the American people and upon the ingenuity of the American people.

What they ask is that we remember one thing only—that China is the Chinese people.

13

Chinese-American Relations

I

THE TIME HAS COME when the relations between the two great peoples of China and the United States should take a step forward. We are at the end of one era and at the beginning of another. The moment between these two eras is plastic. That is, under proper influence the alliance between us may grow stronger and more powerful, so that on the two sides of the world these two nations may stand for the same principles, or under a different influence the United States may be drawn toward Europe rather than toward China, even toward empire rather than toward the freedom of peoples.

For the good not only of China and the United States therefore, but for the good of all peoples and for the cause

The first of the two statements included together here was a confidential memorandum to executives of the East and West Association, the second a speech on an unrecorded occasion, both in 1943.

216

of democracy, it would be well if the two great democracies of East and West could be brought into closer knowledge of each other, in order that there may be fuller understanding between the two peoples, with a view to cooperation and mutual assistance.

The present relations between the two countries seem to have reached a stalemate. This is for several reasons, primary among which is the friendship between Roosevelt and Churchill, which has made easier the connections between the British empire and the United States. The effects of this friendship have been augmented by a very persistent and skillful system of propaganda which has permeated, literally, every part of American life, and which has had as its end the creation of popular opinion as well as opinion among leaders, both political and intellectual, that the safety and destiny of the United States are linked primarily with the British empire, because, as the propaganda has it, the British empire is the only force for law and order now existing in the world.

The effects of this propaganda—taken into account with the naturally easygoing American temper, which is still infused with isolationism and an unwillingness to take responsibility for world affairs, and taken into account with the fact that the English language and culture are common to both Britain and the United States—have been to make many Americans, and an increasing number, think that in the present state of chaos, Americans and British had better join together in controlling the future.

There is imminent danger that such feeling may crystallize into actual agreements unless steps are taken in time, and this means, quickly, to introduce new elements and new ideas to the Americans, both to the public and to the leaders in politics and thought. China has a real duty to perform this function, not only for her own good, but for the good of the world at this moment, in order to keep America, with all her power and resources, in the path of true internationalism and world thinking, rather than allowing her powers and resources to be drained off into the narrower channels of regionalism and even empire. Upon this may depend whether the next centuries are to be peaceful and prosperous for all or racked with war and misery.

The propaganda for regionalism has been the easier because of the complete ignorance of the American people concerning the Chinese. This ignorance is appalling and amazing, not only among the ordinary people, who consider the Chinese to be laundrymen or deserting seamen, but in the highest places in Washington, where policies are decided. This ignorance is surpassed only by similar ignorance among the English, who at present influence Americans strongly, so that these two ignorances augment each other and strengthen those who want a special and close alliance between the English-speaking countries.

It is therefore recommended that China undertake at once a program to acquaint the Americans with China and the Chinese people. There is already in the United States a fund of rather vague and somewhat sentimental goodwill toward the Chinese. But this sort of goodwill is unstable unless it becomes also an informed and purposeful goodwill.

As this sentiment now stands, it can be easily turned into dislike by a few unfortunate experiences, such as are inevitable when individuals of different nationalities and races meet each other unprepared and ignorant of each other's natures. Moreover, this goodwill unfortunately has been much influenced by pity, the sort of pity for the poor Chinese which missionaries have instilled into their followers in order to get funds for their work, and which, in later days, the United China Relief has used on a more widespread and even more disastrous scale. It is inevitable that the appeal to give something to China should have had the undesirable effect of making the average American feel that he stands in superior relation to the Chinese. One particularly deplores this effect on schoolchildren, who in being urged to give their pennies to the poor Chinese are being taught attitudes of the giver toward the suppliant, an attitude which will forbid equality even in the next generation of Chinese and Americans.

Therefore, although the general goodwill toward China is here in America, it cannot be counted on in its present sentimental, unstable, and ignorant form. Indeed, not a few events in recent months have already weakened that goodwill. Propaganda working to estrange China and the United States has made the most of these events, as well as of the mistakes of some individual Chinese.

It is all the more urgent, therefore, that China begins now an intelligent and carefully planned program of education of the American people about China and the Chinese.

The following general plan is suggested:

1. The appointment of a small group of highly educated understanding and wise Chinese whose business it would be to become acquainted in a friendly way with American leaders in all walks of life, but particularly in government, in industry, and in forming public opinion. These men would have no duty other than the careful and tactful cultivation of such leaders and the introduction to them, both through conversation and their own personalities, the knowledge about what the Chinese really are and what China really is and can be, particularly in relation to the American future. Much of the reluctance to allow equality to the Chinese in this war has come about through the diffidence of American leaders too ignorant to know what the Chinese are really like, and afraid that they cannot get on with them or understand them. If one of these leaders personally knows, admires, and understands one Chinese, the gate of his mind would be open toward China and all Chinese.

2. The appointment of a very large number of Chinese to speak before schools, labor union groups, women's clubs, men's groups, and the like, on subjects which would interest such groups, varying from the popular and the humorous to the serious and learned. These persons need not be of so high a quality as the first group, but they should be honest, pleasant, and likable, and suited to the audiences before whom they appear. They should all carry constantly in mind that they in their own behavior and appearance are exemplifying China to America and in proportion as Amer-

icans like and trust them, they will like and trust China. These persons could stay a week at a time in schools and colleges or industrial institutions, and could and should utilize all organizations at present friendly toward China.

These two groups of persons should be a working unit. They should meet together occasionally, compare notes, discuss difficulties, and plan future action. They should be of course under government supervision.

3. There are communities, varying in size, of Chinese throughout the United States. These communities now live in almost complete isolation from Americans. They have shown their loyalty toward China by sending large sums there for relief and war purposes. But they have done very little indeed toward making China and Chinese known in the United States. The reasons for this are obvious—Americans have been careless and have allowed segregation and in some cases demanded it. It is the natural instinct for persons of one group, especially a smaller group, to withdraw in a community. Yet these groups of Chinese might do much in the program of education of Americans if they were helped and directed and taught to feel that they performed a duty when they did so. It is suggested that a few competent persons be appointed to organize Chinese communities in the United States for such a share in the general program of education as they are able to make.

In conclusion, it must be said that, unless some such plan for the education of Americans is carried out, it is doubtful whether China will receive the treatment she deserves either in war or in peace. It is not enough to have persons sent here from China to investigate what Americans are thinking and planning and doing. The time has come for China, for her own sake and for the good of the democratic cause throughout the world, to take an active part in informing that thinking, in taking part in that planning, and in sharing in that achievement.

II

The time is past, it seems to me, when there is the slightest value, if there ever was any value, in not speaking truthfully to each other, as Chinese and as Americans. The truth always comes out, anyway. In this day of quick communications everything is known somewhere, and certainly in all important places. Be sure that in China, beginning in Chungking, everything that is done inside Washington's most secret rooms is known and reckoned with, and be sure that in the highest circles of the White House, as well as elsewhere, the facts of China's plans and policies are down in black and white. Nothing is hidden anywhere these days—there are no "secrets" as there used to be secrets in the old days, when months and miles lay between the nations.

Yet there is ignorance in the most important place—that is, among our people. Governments and diplomats are in full possession of facts, and big business interests hire many men who do nothing but ferret for facts. Only the people are kept uninformed. Biased newspapers suppress some facts and enlarge others, a timid radio service avoids mention, again and again, of the very things upon which our future depends. It is time that peoples dare to speak out to each across the barriers. We have nothing to fear from one another—on the contrary, it is only to each other that we can look for help against imperialisms, political and economic, which threaten us. The world will not be a good place for any people until it is a place good for all. That seems an obvious thing to say, and yet is unheeded, as so much truth is unheeded.

And yet we can scarcely have this cooperation unless we have the necessary knowledge upon which to base such cooperation. It is essential to China and the United States to be allies in the peace. It is essential for the continuance of our American way of life that we have facing us across this Pacific Ocean a great democratic nation, whose principles are our principles, and whose government has the same aims that ours has. China is the one nation upon whom we can and must count, the only nation which has had no ambitions for territory or political power over others. If China remains our friend, then Asia is our friend. If China is not our friend, then we face a dangerous future.

Knowing the warm and even affectionate attitude which the American people have toward the Chinese, you will wonder that there is any reason why today I should repeat what we all know—that our country and China must be allies in the peace. Surely, you will say, this is what we all desire and even take as a matter of course.

But there is reason for my dwelling upon the necessity today, and the reason is that I do not believe that the average American has any idea of the real situation existing today between ourselves and China. We, here, are in a haze of goodwill toward China. The extremely successful United China Relief Drive, the visit of the beautiful and dramatic Madame Chiang, combined with our historic good feelings toward China and the pleasant personal friendships that many of us have enjoyed with individual Chinese, surround us with a bright fog. The truth is that all is not well between our two countries, and for our own sakes we ought to know it.

What are the relations between our two countries?

They are increasingly less cordial. The Chinese have always considered us as a friend. How powerful a friend they have not been able to estimate. Historically, our policy of the "Open Door in China" has been one which they have appreciated, while they placed upon it a somewhat lower value than we ourselves have done. The "Open Door" policy kept China from being actually partitioned during the years when she was weakest, but it did not keep her from suffering many grievous oppressions from European and other nations. Wilson literally gave China to Japan when he recognized Japan's pretensions to special rights. Therefore, the first world war gave Japan the hold upon China which she wanted. When Japan seized Manchuria, our protest was noble but ineffectual. Like the "Open Door" policy, it sounded good, but did not really prevent robbery going on. It makes me think of a kindly, middle-aged gentleman I once knew in a town in north China where a magistrate was trying to set up a modern police force. This gentleman volunteered for the service and looked wonderful in his new uniform. But a few days afterward I found him back at his old job of public letter writer. "How is this?" I asked him. "I thought you were the new policeman."

"So I was," he said, "and I did not mind walking around carrying a gun. But then I found that I was expected to fire the gun also, and so I resigned."

Our position toward China has been much like this. We have been quite willing to wear a uniform and carry a gun, but when the reality of firing the gun fell upon us, we resigned.

Of course we *have* been very kind to China. We have poured missionary funds and personnel into her for years, and now a great stream of relief money flows out toward her. I think the time has come for us to realize that this is not now what China wants. I am reminded of one of my sons, a seven-year-old of extremely practical mind. Last Christmas, surrounded by the gifts of a large and too generous family, he found the one thing he wanted, an engine, and said bluntly, "All these other things I don't want—only this one thing."

This realism was quite apparent even in Madame Chiang, when she said with equal bluntness, "I did not come to America to beg for anything," and when with steadfastness she refused to take part in any relief-money raising. I will give you an example nearer home. In a Hollywood studio a picture is being made of my book *Dragon Seed*. I was there the other day to look at some of the scenes, and someone responsible said to me, "It is a great regret to us that we are having to leave out some things that make the Chinese character the most appealing and even endearing. We pointed this out to the young Chinese official who is censoring the picture for his government, but he said, 'We had rather do without American sympathy if it implies that there is any inferiority in us, however naïve and appealing it makes us appear.' "

While the American people are thinking rather fondly and affectionately of the Chinese people, therefore, the Chinese are not thinking in the same way of us. This is a new sharpness in China toward us, a new pride, an excessive sensitivity, and a guardedness which ought not to be necessary if there were trust. I think we ought to know this, to know its causes, and to reckon with its effects if it cannot be changed.

Why, you will ask, should China have this new attitude toward us? I will only enumerate the contributing causes which must be familiar to you: our foreign policy in the past, which, while amiable, was not strong; our failure to insist upon our own stand in regard to Manchuria; our shipping of munitions material to Japan when we knew Japan was using it against China; our failure to hold back Japan in the South Pacific; our failure to send military aid since in any useful amounts, so that lend-lease has been of little value to China; our almost studied insults toward Chinese officials, particularly military officials in Washington. All these were, and are, simply reasons for one great conviction which has been steadily growing in the minds of the Chinese until now I am afraid that it is tending to become unalterable. The conviction is that Washington takes directions from London.

I am well aware that when I go on talking about this, I am not merely twisting the lion's tail, I am literally putting my head in the lion's mouth. But I beg of you to remember that I am only telling you what I know the Chinese are thinking. Do not blame me, please, for what they think. I am not saying that they are right or wrong.

Now there is no use in hiding the fact that the Chinese feel very bitterly toward the British empire, partly because, with all Asia, they are sick to death of foreign imperialisms and partly because they have suffered from British imperialism particularly. They are on the side of the democracies in this war—rather, on the side of democracy. But they make no pretense at hiding the fact that they hold British imperialism as dangerous as the Japanese. Read Lin Yutang's last book and see what they mean. It is not just one angry man crying aloud in that book. It is how the Chinese feel. They feel cheated in this war because Churchill has declared himself plainly for England's old empire. They are angered at what happened in India. Generalissimo Chiang Kai-shek, during the period of the Cripps Mission, himself cabled Churchill begging a generous settlement with India, for the sake of all Asia, and Churchill did not reply. When again Chiang Kai-shek cabled, Churchill replied haughtily to the British Ambassador in Chungking that he did not wish to be troubled further by these cables. There has been no sign whatever as yet that Hong Kong would be restored to the Chinese, and this the Chinese take as a portent of the future.

However rightly or wrongly, the Chinese are convinced from many instances which they consider proof that our British ally wants a weak China and does not want too weak a Japan.

To this end Chinese believe that our British ally has deliberately sought to malign China in Washington, to minimize her efforts in the war where such belittling would have the most telling effect—namely, in the ears of the highest military men and of the President. To this they attribute our policy toward China, which has steadily been one of ignoring, except by occasional outbursts of congratulatory talk, China's increasingly desperate situation. China believes, too, that our British ally, in her determination to pry China and the United States apart, has again and again deliberately placed a false emphasis upon the division between the governing party in China and the Communist Party, so that military aid which China might have had has not been sent because of rumors that Chang Kai-shek would use them against the Eighth Route Army rather than against Japan.

So strong did such rumors become that some of us who were known to be friends of China felt compelled to face them and distinguish between true and false and place the blame where it belonged, and certainly not wholly upon the Chinese.

For there was some truth in the rumors, the same amount of truth in similar rumors that could be spread abroad about any country. We all know that this war is being fought not only against fascism abroad. An intense struggle is going on in England and in the United States, too, the struggle between strong, centralized reactionary forces and the forces for democracy. Churchill does not speak for the whole of England, but only for those now in power. The opposition is alive.

This same intense struggle is going on in China, too, not between the Communists and the Kuomingtang primarily, but between the reactionary forces and democratic forces, both inside and outside the government and the party. That struggle is not yet decided in China any more than it is here —perhaps it cannot be decided in China until it is decided here. For I believe that literally the future of the world will be decided here in our own land and, I grieve to say, by people too ignorant as yet to know when they next vote that they are shaping the world by that vote. If the reactionary forces in this country win, with their old prejudice against the man of Asia, and if these forces here join with the governing element in England to make a narrow alliance of our two countries, China may well turn away from democracy in a world lost to democracy. In that dark day she will be our enemy and not our friend, and out of an Asia that we will quickly come to fear with terror and dismay, the white man will meet his doom.

I tremble when I think of it. I am not a timid person. I have faced death more than once and not been afraid. But I confess to you I wake up in the night now and know what fear is. For I do not like what is happening. I do not like it when I hear Chinese say we Americans are following Churchill like a big pleasant dog. I know how they feel toward Churchill and I don't want them to feel that way toward us. Indeed it is not necessary for us who have never loved empire anywhere, or wanted empire for ourselves, to suffer now the burden of an empire in whose profits we have not shared.

I am not anti-British, I love England, its land and its people. But I see—I believe—that the day has come for the end of empire as a principle of government over peoples. I love my own people above all others. Not even for the sake of our great ally, England, can I refrain from pointing out to you, who are my fellow citizens, that for our own sakes, for the sake of our country, we must form an independent policy toward Asia and particularly toward China; a policy not dictated by the need and determination to maintain an empire, but shaped solely by our own democratic principles and our belief in the equality of peoples and their right to the same freedom which we enjoy.

It is not yet too late to state this independent policy and to act upon it for our own salvation. It is not too late to insist on China's equal partnership with ourselves and Britain and Russia. But unless we take a stand soon it will be too late, for as things are going now, China will not have a real voice at the peace table. If she is not a full partner, then it can be guaranteed that there will be no peace, not even a short one. Our men must not even lay down their arms. There will not be time to rest—we must stay armed. For if China is not heard at the peace table, Asia will burst into flames someday, too soon.

What can we do? Well, just wake ourselves up and then demand a new policy toward China. Washington is still very sensitive to people's outcries, and particularly to the outcries of the people along our Pacific Coast. This broad strip of earth facing the Pacific is, I believe, the most important part of our country. As you decide concerning Asia, the country will decide. You can make of California a barrier between Asia and ourselves or a gateway. Barriers make wars, but gateways make peace. For people go in and out and know each other as friends and neighbors.

14

East and West

IN THE MIDST OF the war there is beginning to grow something new in the hearts of the peoples of all nations. The peoples are impatient for the war to be ended because they feel something new is ahead, an experience which they are eager to begin. What it is none knows, for the stirring of rebirth is not yet a knowledge so much as it is an instinct. Victory for the peoples in this war is necessary, for the peoples must be free or the rebirth will not come. Every era of renaissance has come out of new freedoms for peoples. The coming renaissance will be greater than any in human history, for this time all the peoples of the earth will share in it. Freedom for all must be the principle of the peace that the atmosphere may be right for the full flowering of this rebirth.

What has led us to this moment?

First, the development of science—science applied to

Article in American Mercury, *May, 1945. Copyright, 1945, by American Mercury.*

swift ships, to airplanes, to motor vehicles of every kind; science, building new roads in all the countries, brought the peoples closer, not only the peoples of different countries but the people within the limits of a single nation. In China the people of different provinces were as alien as though they lived in separate nations until steamships on the rivers and motor vehicles on new roads brought them face to face. In Africa, in South America, in Russia, people are living through the same experience of learning to know their own countrymen. But ships and airplanes have tied the continents together, too, and have bridged the nations.

Second came the war to hasten the process of acquaintance. It might have taken another century to do what the war has done in a few years. The war has forced peoples together as allies or enemies. The peoples of China and America and Britain have been compelled to know the peoples of Japan and Germany from an evil experience but they have been compelled to know them. The peoples of China and America have been forced to new knowledge of each other as allies. Russia's people, too, have had to be known anew. But it is a hasty and incomplete knowledge, this knowledge which war has forced upon the peoples. It is like a short course in college, taken under the compulsion of an examination. There is no depth to it. The abnormal, unhealthy experience of war has given them only glimpses of each other fighting, in deep distress, wounded, dying. The peoples have not had the experience yet of living together.

But the war has done this, at least: it has created a desire among peoples for further knowledge. The peoples of the United Nations look toward each other with new interest and wonder and hope. Having fought side by side to victory, why then, they are asking, can we not carry on this relationship in times of peace? It is out of this wonder and this hope that the rebirth will come, the new Renaissance, the greatest that mankind has yet known.

Any new birth comes from a cooperative process, a fertilizing and a fostering. The Renaissance of the Middle Ages in Europe came from such cooperation. The age preceding it had been a sterile one, in spite of Europe's riches. Something was lacking, something new to inspire and energize. The opening of routes to the East provided the stimulus. The rich soil of Europe was impregnated with new knowledge from the East, and out of the union there came such a flowering of the human mind that men have looked back to it with wonder ever since. The imagination of the peoples of Europe was stirred, they woke and began to create new arts and new crafts, to undertake new industries, and to shape a new life which penetrated into every phase of society. No one escaped the benefits of the Renaissance.

In that age it was the peoples of the East who gave it to the peoples of the West. The East was not stirred in return. The life of the Eastern peoples was already rich, so much richer than that of Europe that they could give out of their abundance of culture and learning and achievement, and feel no need of return.

But there was still no real communication between the

peoples. The life of the world, East and West, went on, separated by seas and distance. The impetus given to Europe continued to flower over a long period and spread to the American hemisphere. Now it was Asia that grew sterile with age and isolation and now it was the West's turn to impregnate the East.

The rebirth came to the East when steamships were invented. Ships went to China and to India and to Japan in numbers greater than ever before, carrying traders and missionaries and diplomats. The East was unwilling and unresponsive in those days. The peoples of China and Japan and India did not want to be disturbed. They had lived in their own silence so long, and the newcomers were noisy and boisterous and arrogant. Yet what they did not welcome they had to accept. Life forced them into life again, however unwillingly.

But all birth is unwilling. The child in the womb struggles against being born. The old, accustomed to age, struggle against death, the new form of life. Thus rebirth came to the East and the peoples woke and began to live in the modern world, a world full of conflicts and wars, but alive. Revolutions in China and in Russia, unrest and discontent in India, an angry militarism in Japan, these have been the signs of awakening peoples of the East.

Now world war has thrown the doors open wide. We know that when the war is won there will be no more barriers of sea and distance between us. We know that swifter ships and more ships than ever before will be daily, hourly, crossing the seas. We know that in the skies the great airplanes will be speeding from people to people. Already those who build the airplanes are beginning to quarrel over the airways—as though the skies belonged to any, and not to all!

The peoples, still in the throes of this most bitter war, are looking ahead and seeing and feeling the possibilities of all that can be, if there is freedom for it to be. Communication between them; travel, quick and cheap; the interchange of the treasures of merchandise, of new flowers and plants and trees; the even more important exchange of thoughts and new ways, the pooling of that which human beings have learned in the centuries lived apart—all this the peoples are already thinking about and imagining.

This rebirth will be the greatest of all, for there is more equality now between the peoples than there has ever been before. In the Renaissance of the Middle Ages it was the East that gave to the West. In the modern Renaissance of Asia it was the West that gave to the East. But now each has something to give to the other, and from this mutual need and mutual richness there will spring, if the times are free, life for mankind richer and better than anything we have yet known.

What has the West to give the East? A better physical life, a practical knowledge of medicine and hygiene and of all the ways in which science can improve health and environment, an improved industrial life, industries which are the creation of science applied to man's needs for work and for finished materials and for the objects he uses every day for convenience and pleasure. Most important of all, the

West can give the East a technique of modern democracy, which provides for the individual a method of expressing his own opinion and wielding his own power in the government of his people.

What has the East to give the West?

Deep knowledge of how people can live together happily and with mutual respect, the Chinese philosophy of reasonableness so practically applied by China's people for ages, and the value of the individual human spirit which has been its fruit; the deep belief in man's relation to God and eternity, that belief in which the peoples of India live and move and have their being, and the noble patience which has been the fruit of it; the loyalty and high sense of duty which the people of Japan have developed, even when the object of that loyalty has been unworthy; the conviction of the equality of all races upon which Russia alone out of all the peoples has founded her new nation. We of the West need spiritual enrichment today as never before. In our preoccupation with the wonders of science applied to materials we have forgotten that man does not live by bread alone. These words came out of the East two thousand years ago and it is the East who has never forgotten them and who must teach us again their truth.

East and West today the peoples need each other. Nothing must be allowed to keep us apart, neither the greed of merchants nor the prejudices of the arrogant. The plain peoples of the earth must find each other, they must discover that they are alike in their simple and deep desires. East and West we do long for the same things, for love and home and children, for work whose fruit will feed the family; for peace, for freedom in which to live and think and grow. These are not impossible longings, not dreams that cannot be realized. They are the rights of all mankind. But the plain peoples must work together to achieve them, and give them to each other, or they will not have them. And how can they work together except as they cease to be strangers and become friends?

It is the duty of all, therefore, to open every door of approach, to cultivate every source of knowledge, to try to find out by any means possible, the ways and habits and beliefs and hopes of other peoples not his own, to the end that with common knowledge and in mutual understanding, all peoples may work together for a good and peaceful world.

15

Letter to My Chinese Friend

"To meet ten thousand changing circumstances with an unchanging self"—this is one of those
seemingly simple sayings of which your literature and life
are so rich. One speaks them easily and quickly, and it is
not difficult to understand them. And yet the more one
ponders upon them the more they mean, and the more one
comes to comprehend their meaning. For of course this
saying can be comprehended and practiced only by the
mature soul, whether it is the soul of an individual or of a
people. Youth changes with every circumstance. His soul
is unfixed and unshaped. He does not know what he is and
he is constantly trying to find something fixed and secure
in circumstances around him, whereby he can make himself
secure. It is only when he comes to see that there will never
be anything fixed and secure in outward circumstances that

Written in the mid-1940's.

he begins to see that it is himself he must shape into change-lessness. But this is the process of growing, and when he has reached his goal of an unchanging soul, he is no longer young.

Nations, too, repeat the process. You are old and wise and we are young and not wise. As a people we are still changing constantly with every circumstance in the swiftly changing world about us and it does not yet appear what we shall be. Our main efforts are still being put on trying to fix the shape of the world, so that we may be secure. The Monroe Doctrine, for instance, was an effort to fix the shape of the world about us. We were afraid to be entangled in the changefulness of the world and so we said we would not be entangled. What we could not understand was that, first, we could not escape entanglement in the world so long as we all breathe the same air, and second, that we need not fear entanglement if we had an unchanging soul of our own.

We were entangled in the first world war, and again we were afraid and we withdrew from the changing circumstances about us after that war was fought. This more than anything explains our refusal to join the League of Nations. We were insecure in our own national soul, and we were afraid of a world so new, or of taking part in the shape of that world. Like children we wanted to keep the walls we knew high around us, and to ignore as far as possible and, we hoped, utterly, whatever went on outside those walls. What we could not or would not foresee was that no walls

240

can be high enough or strong enough these days to keep
out the world. They are battered down by bombs from the
sky, and who can shut out the sky and live?

These physical barriers have failed us. You may now
expect to see us begin to rear other barriers to make ourselves safe until our soul is established. Trade barriers will
be strengthened, immigration barriers will be emphasized,
and it is possible that even our prejudices will increase.
Do not expect of us that we will be leaders in the world
yet. We are still too young. We may have and probably will
have great daring, great inventiveness, and the highest
skills in the physical techniques of science. We are quite
sure of ourselves on these visible and tangible grounds.
But we are less sure of our soul today than ever, and to
guard our soul you will find us lagging in human ways. I
say we may, therefore, become more and more prejudiced
against certain peoples. I believe this prejudice will not
follow strictly the lines of color, and for this we have to
thank you.

For in this war, both by reason of your own great bravery and the assiduity with which friends of China have
urged your worth, the people of my country are prepared
to break down their own prejudice against color in your
single case. The fact that they are willing to do this in your
single case will probably mean that they will strengthen their
old prejudices in the cases of other peoples. That is, you
have behaved in ways which they greatly admire. Your
courage, your steadfastness, your unchanging soul in the

241

face of the terrible changes in the world and in your country have touched our sentimental hearts. We are ready to declare that you are allies worthy of us. There is no doubt that we had rather you were white, but since you are not, we will accept that fact, and we will sing your praises and accord you every favor. You must now prepare for a period of friendship from us which will tax to the utmost your unchanging soul. We are now ready to love you and hate all others. We shall hate the Japanese of course in proportion as we love you, and you will not mind this. But our hatred will extend into peace and probably will keep Asia in a turmoil for a while, because we will stick closer to you than to a brother, and this will not build for peace with Japan when the time comes when we must make peace. Neither for your sake will we love the dark people any better elsewhere who have behaved so truculently to the English during this war, and we shall be glad to punish them by our dislike. And the more dislike we have for other peoples the more love we shall have for you. This is a touching sign of our youth—that we are not yet able to have a feeling for humanity. We must love this man and hate that one—we cannot grant that all men are human.

Now two things must be said about this necessity of ours to love and to hate. For the time being you will profit by it. You will receive benefits from our love for you. The unequal treaties which have been such a shame to us and such a burden to you have now been abrogated—or it is promised that they will be abrogated. Do not imagine that they were abrogated because we do not believe in unequal treaties. They were abrogated because we now love you, and loving you, we want to do all we can for you. You must not be misled into thinking that we make such changes on the ground of justice to all men. No, if we make the change in our outward behavior, it will be only because we love you so much. We will not hate others less.

But it would be foolish to deny the fact that it is a great experience for us to love a people of a different color than our own, and a people of Oriental origin rather than European. This in itself is a fact that will change us and change the whole world. Even though we do not so mean it. The fact that we can love you whose skin is invariably yellow and whose eyes and hair invariably black means that we have acknowledged that it is possible to love persons of such invariable coloring invariably different from our own. It may make it possible someday for us to enlarge our love to include yet another people of color not like our own. Of course that will take a long time since we are moving toward it by this childlike method of loving one people because of characteristics of that people, rather than proceeding from the universal principle that all people are human beings and must be so considered and treated.

But we are too young to act from principle. Our behavior is motivated solely on the grounds of our prejudices. Yet what I am trying to say is simply that the breaking down of prejudice at one point makes it possible to break down the prejudice at another point, provided there is something that makes an appeal stronger than the prejudice. And yet even as the prejudices break we must expect a strengthening of the prejudices that are left. Because we love you so ardently these days, the dark people must expect greater hatred from us.

I heard a wise Jew say this the other day. Of all our people only the Jews are wise and old, and it may be that is why we do not love them much. Youth and age cannot live together very well under our roof. Your people are, of course, all born old.

Well, this Jew had come to a meeting of the dark people. These dark people were sad and angry at the treatment which they are receiving these days in our own country. It is worse on the whole than they had during the last war, and yet that is natural in the state of the world today. But they are a young people too, and they cannot understand why this should be so, and they are protesting.

At this meeting one of the dark men turned to the Jew and he said, "You are one of the oppressed peoples too, and why do not you join with us, in order that we may all throw off oppression together?" To which the Jew replied with a sad, wise look, "Ah, but we know that insofar as you are loved we will be increasingly hated."

I thought to myself, "How well he knows us!" For here within our own country it is true that if our hatred should turn to the Jews, we will be more kind to the dark people. But if our hatred should turn to the dark people, the Jews will escape more lightly, even as in the world outside because we love you we shall probably hate some other people.

Now all this of course is simply the evidence of our youth. We have not an unchanging soul. The soul of our people is not yet formed or even presaged. We do not know what we are. We do not even know what we want to be. The unfortunate part of it is that we are in a position in this moment of . the world's history of great potential power. We are young, we are strong, we are rich, and we can, because of our power, affect the world in ways which we are not fit to affect it. We are like a strong young boy with a gun who, because of his strength and because of his gun, has the possibility of power over people much better and much wiser than he. What we will do with our strength and our gun remains to be seen. But for the moment we will not turn them against you because we have decided to love you.

But the world will have to suffer with us and through us while we are establishing our national soul. Do not expect to see us either rational or wise. Do not expect to see us pursuing a steady and unchanging policy of any sort. Nothing steady and unchanging can come out of us for a long time.

You are so wise that I may speak to you as frankly as I like. I beg you that you will understand us as we are, forgive us our youthful arrogance and boasting, and overlook our changefulness, and use your present position in our affections for the good of the world. When we come to the peace table together, the men of my country and the men of yours, do not look to our men for a wisdom which they

245

do not and cannot possess. Do not wait to be led by them. But remembering your own great age, let your wisdom shine forth as a light for us all. In that lamp of your wisdom burns the oil of human understanding. You know the heart of mankind and we do not know. Even though you have suffered so much from this war, I do not doubt for one moment that when you sit at the peace table you will be able to think of the Japanese as human beings who must also live in the world. But we shall not be able so to think. There are many of us who think that after this war we must really exterminate our present enemies. It is you who must be ready always to point out that this would only mean eternal war.

And of course you must remember that our intense hatred at the peace table will not last either. It would of course be very wise to postpone entirely that peace table for, say, a period of five years. During that time trade would be resumed and people would have a chance to see what natural shapes the world will take. Then we could base the peace terms upon those natural shapes and perhaps it would last longer, at least, than it has in the ten treaties made in the last three centuries in Europe. But it is not likely that we can be wise enough for that. The people who are now crying out for a fiercer and fiercer war will also cry out for a fierce peace.

Yet the fierce peace we made at Versailles did not last. We quickly ceased to hate the Germans merely because we turned our mind to other things. An old hate is something like an old love. It is hard to inflame it again, however hard we blow upon the ashes. It is well for us that we have this new enemy, the Japanese, to hate. We can hate them so much that our cup of hatred brims and runs over.

What we are too young to understand, of course, is that even the rush of our new hatred cannot compare in power and cool ferocity with the sort of determination you have against the enemy. The passionate anger of a boy cannot compare with the steady implacability of a mature man toward one whom he is determined to crush.

I read a discussion in one of our weeklies not long ago between two distinguished persons on whether or not it is necessary to hate the enemy in order to fight him successfully. One side was argued by one of our great citizens, a woman elderly and wise because she is one who has an unchanging soul. The other side was argued by a young man whose soul is a will-of-the-wisp. Each argued well according to the light his soul gave. I read it all with a smile. For of course the question cannot be argued and the answer is simple. One must have hatred because otherwise he has nothing else to fight with, and he must have hatred at least to bolster his courage and put energy in his arm. But the wise one does not need hatred. He fights out of the deep unchanging determination of his being against what he thinks is wrong, and of these two the dangerous one is the wise one. For he fights without hatred and so he is the most bitter enemy in the world.

I know that it is because you do not hate the Japanese as human beings that you have withstood them so successfully all these years. Hatred would not have had such

247

strength. Fear can change hatred, and defeat can change hatred. But nothing can change your unchanging soul. You are not fighting the people of Japan. You are pitting your soul against theirs. And of the two, theirs will break first, for it too is a younger soul, and it is fed upon angers and prejudices and personal desires and greeds. It proceeds more quickly to single successes than yours does, but yours is stronger at the end.

Do not, of course, count on our always loving you. It will take your wisdom and all your canny skill in human relations to cement our present warm love into the steady lasting bonds of understanding friendship. At present our people are really completely ignorant of your people. They impulsively pour out money for you because they love you, not because they understand you. If they hear you are hungry and that you are wounded and ill, they put their hands into their pockets at once. But that means nothing for the future except that the door is open into our hearts. You may come in, but whether you stay or not depends on how wise a guest you are. If you press too much upon us, if you presume upon our love, we will return hastily to our old prejudices. The prejudices are not dead, they are only sleeping, even in your case. And in all other cases they are very much alive.

But because we love you, even for the moment, we are very much in your hands. You can, if you are wise, use our love for the good of all, or only for the good of yourselves. You know, of course, what happens when love is used for selfish ends—it dies quickly. We are an idealistic people as well as a materialistic one—I told you our soul is very changing and it changes not only from hour to hour, but it is changeful in its contradictions at the same time. Our idealism is shown in the fact that we continue to love those whom we can also admire for their goodness, and we cease to love where we cannot admire. Just now, as I said, we admire you enormously, especially because you have fought Japan so bravely and so steadfastly. And your friends among us have increased our love by making known your other fine qualities, the humanism of your philosophers and the high civilization of your citizens, even though you have not stressed literacy for technical development as much as we have. We love you, that is, although seventy-five percent of your people are illiterate, and we hate Japan although ninety-five percent of her people are literate. That is because we believe wholeheartedly that your people are good and Japanese people are bad, and now you know and I know that not all your people are good, and not all Japanese are bad. Indeed even my people, or most of them, would acknowledge this as an intellectual fact, but as a fact it does not reach their hearts. And we are all heart, we Americans, except where we are all head. The connections between are closed off. Those connections, of course, in you run freely, although not directly. In you they go through the belly, also, so that belly, brain, and heart are all working together sensibly.

But nothing confuses us more than knowing that good and bad are to be found in the same people. We know it but we don't want to believe it and so we do not believe it.

It is another evidence of our youth that we do not believe what is but often what we want to think is. And we like to know a thing so that we can forget it. If we know that you are good and the Japanese are bad, then we can forget it and go on and act in the simple ways of loving you and hating the Japanese. It would upset us very much if we found that in you there are things that are bad and that we cannot love, and it would upset us equally if we found that there were good things in the Japanese that we could not hate. It would really turn the world upside down for us just now to discover that we might possibly love the Japanese. Of course after the war is over, the world will turn anyway, but just now we have stopped the world from its turning. Japan is down and you are up.

Now you will see your dangerous position. Actually it will be easier for Japan than you. Love is so dangerously easy to lose—much more easily lost than hatred. As many of your people are bad as there are to be found in other countries, including our own. And your civilization is far from perfect. Its strength is in the reality of its foundations. It is that reality which makes your unchanging soul. Our foundations are still shifting and much of them is unreal because it is not based on the solid rock of universality, and of the understanding of the common nature of man. But you have the soundest foundations of all civilization. The unsound ones fell in Greece and Rome. Ours will fall too, of course, unless we can find the solid rock. Perhaps you can show us the way to that rock.

But to get back to what I was saying, the danger in our

relations with you will be that because of our love we shall ask of you the impossible individual perfections which you have not. Venality, nepotism, and cruelty are some of your faults. They are not greater or less than our own in quality, though perhaps because of your age and your numbers, they are greater in quantity. That is, the bad men here are just as bad as the ones in your country, but perhaps we have fewer bad men here in proportion to the others, simply because we are a young people and we demand a black or white sort of morality in our citizens, whereas you have lived so long that you condone a certain amount of black and white in the same individual.

We are young, we are young, and if you would understand us and our ways, then study a lad of fourteen and fifteen and see what his ways are and how willful are his thoughts. But he must be a strong and passionate lad, not a book-loving one, not a scholar. Let him be impetuous and hungry—and handsome.

16

Some American Myths About the Chinese

OUR AMERICAN POLICY toward China today is in an interesting state of flux. No one knows quite what it should be and, therefore, no one can do more than guess what it is going to be. It may be wise enough for us to do nothing for a brief space, during perplexity, so far as China is concerned, but equally wise would it be to do some preparatory attic cleaning meanwhile in our own minds, for there is an amazing amount of trash in our mental attics when it comes to the Chinese. Age-old fragments of misinformation still clutter our thinking and added to the heavy accumulation is new misinformation, ladled out by persons who have been in China very recently, very briefly, and who have gone there with a job to do, a purpose to accomplish—a fatal atmosphere in which to approach any people. No one who goes with a mission to a people ever learns anything about

Article in The New York Times Magazine, *October 23, 1949 (under title "Our Dangerous Myths About China"). Copyright assigned to Pearl S. Buck, 1950.*

them, neither what they are nor what they want. It is inevitable that most missions, religious, political, and military, are usually failures.

It will not be possible very soon to clear our attics entirely of the residues of a century or so, but certain large and cumbersome myths might be cast into the bottom of the sea for good and all. First of all, I would reject the myth that China's basic problem is hunger. It will be a myth difficult to relinquish, for it is an easy explanation of China's troubles. A hungry man can always be handed bread and the bread then becomes a debt. Did I not feed you when you were hungry? Thus bread turns into stone. The actual fact is that hunger is not China's chief problem. Anyone who lived in China before the last war knows that in spite of the overthrow of one government and the setting up of a new military government under Generalissimo Chiang Kai-shek, never thoroughly accomplished, and in spite of consequent continued regional civil war, the Chinese fed themselves heartily and well, as they have done for a very long time, indeed. True, there were occasional famines, of which Americans heard very much through other Americans, mostly kindhearted missionaries. But these famines were not the result of basic food shortage. They were caused by catastrophe, by flood or drought. Flood and drought are not always preventable but they are always local. China's vast territory, much larger than ours, can easily remedy any local famine, were there roads enough. Lack of communications is a basic problem in China and has been for a very long time. In my own experience it was often cheaper and actually easier in some famines to ship wheat across the Pacific Ocean from the United States and Canada than it was to bring it over three hundred miles of Chinese country road on donkey and man back.

During the eight years of the last war, of course, many farm families fled and the food situation was disrupted, and local disruptions will continue until the country has peace. Yet in spite of war and disturbance the Chinese farmer even now produces vast quantities of food which he would be glad to market more widely, were it possible. The Chinese earth is rich in food production, and the Chinese farmer is skilled in conserving the soil. The Chinese are indeed farmers of forty centuries and there they have much to teach the rest of the world. They need help in scientific seed selection and in disease and insect control, which can easily be given them. The primary need of the Chinese farmer, therefore, is not food but more markets for the food he has.

The abundance of food production in China is more than the result of necessity. The Chinese are extremely modern in their outlook on life. Centuries before Hemingway set the fashion for naturalism before America's young men and women, the Chinese were naturalistic to their very marrow. Every function of life was meant to be enjoyed. Therefore, food was much more than a necessity—it became an art, in production, in cookery, in eating, and an astounding plenty and variety of foods were developed. Those who have wandered over China will remember the wonder of the markets even in remote little inland towns. Tubers of

land and water, roots of delicacy and flavor, green vegetables infinitely more in number than are eaten or even
known by Americans, melons of every color and texture and
flavor, both as fruit and vegetables, meats fresh and dried in
a score of ways, proteins we do not suspect from beans
and peas made into vegetable cheeses and cured or eaten
fresh, seafood of every variety, river fish of every size and
sort, the nuts, the sweets, the fruits—I wonder why we do
not have loquats, those delicious golden fruits of spring, and
why we do not have pumeloes, so much better than grape-
fruit and greater in variety, and why we do not have the many
kinds of persimmons that the Chinese have? The big persimmons of the north dried for sweetmeats and dusted with pow-
dered sugar surpass any figs or dates, though the Chinese
honey dates, delicately slit with needles and then preserved
in honey, are the finest in the world. No one who has eaten
for years in China, north and south and all around, in city
and village, can believe that the Chinese are hungry or that
they need food—primarily, that is. Take bread alone—in
comparison to the poor pastry product which Americans
eat for their daily bread, what joy is to be found in the many
varieties of Chinese bread—the baked, the browned in deep
vegetable oil, the steamed in vast trays set into the huge
iron cauldron; bread in loaves, bread in cakes, bread
delicately filled with bean vermicelli and spinach, bread
filled with flavored pork bits, bread filled with dates crushed
in red sugar.

No, I flout the idea that the Chinese are permanently
hungry and that their hunger is a world problem. I have

breakfasted in southern villages with the poor and found delicious the bowls of rice gruel and salted vegetables and fish, or in north China the thin sheet of unsalted bread wrapped about a fresh stalk of garlic. I have eaten a bowl of homemade noodles flavored with soy sauce and sesame oil in a poor wayside inn and I have eaten official feasts of many courses, and all are delicious and abundant. The Chinese not only eat well, they eat heartily. They are heavy feeders, especially those who work at physical labor, which is most of the people.

Not food, but roads are what the Chinese need, roads whereby to share with each other their own plenty. A network of good roads and freight vehicles to use them, combined with a few main railroad lines and some refrigerator cars, and China's famines would be wiped from the record.

Allied to this primary myth about the hungry Chinese is another—that much of China's land is owned by a few big landlords and that here lies the strength of the Communist movement. Actually, I suppose no country in the world has proportionately as few big landlords as China. A man who owns five hundred acres there is rare indeed. Even a hundred acres is monstrous. The average Chinese farm is a little over five acres and the land is too much divided, rather than too little. The rule of primogeniture has never been followed. A man's land belongs to his sons. As many as can make a living on it divide it up into parcels. The others find jobs in neighboring towns or become tenant workers for well-to-do farmers. The land is never idle. Sowing follows harvest and skill from experience maintains the soil. Public health will teach the farmer in mid and south China not to use human manure directly upon crops to be eaten green or slightly cooked. Otherwise, he understands his job and does it well and usually upon his own land.

The Communists in China, contrary to the myth, will find the large number of individual farms an obstacle. The Chinese have a strong property sense, especially about family land. However far a man may wander, however long he stays away, he looks back to the few patriarchal acres as home. Collective farms will go against his grain, indeed. I doubt they can ever be attempted in China on any scale.

Having mentioned Communism, let me wipe the dust from still another myth—a recent one. It is that all Chinese in the Nationalist ranks are corrupt. This is not true. Many good and able and strong men are Nationalists. That they were not able to prevail in time to prevent the Communist attack we Americans ought to understand well enough. In both our own major parties there are better men than we have usually put to public use. Even our excellent democratic processes do not always allow our best men and women to reach the seats of power. How much less, then, could they emerge in the Nationalist Party in China, where the democratic processes were never set up! To the very last, the Nationalist government has remained a military one, and civilians of whatever strength are powerless to prevail. Many honest and true men spent hours innumerable with President Chiang, earnestly begging him to allow them to bring in the essential reforms. Perhaps he is not to be judged too harshly when, after having more than once given a wavering consent, he withdrew his promises. His has always been a precarious place, won by battle and not by the choice of the people. He has never quite had the courage to put his sword aside and take up the far more skillful and difficult business of serving his people. In this has been his weakness and the cause of his downfall. Yet he himself is not a bad man—far from it. He is personally austere, he does not love luxury. But he was weaned on war, militarism is all he knows, and it alone he trusts. He was not able to understand even the good civilians in his own ranks, much less those who came from abroad. Bear in mind that he has never seen a democracy at work. It might have been wise to have shown him the brighter spots of the American democracy. The real weakness of the Nationalists has not been corruption, primarily, but a leadership which has not understood the modern world, and which produced a stalemate atmosphere, in which corruption always breeds.

Here I had better drag out still another myth, again not ancient. It is the myth that China is now certainly going Communist. I am not one of these who comfort myself with the pap that the Chinese Communist leaders today are not really Communist. They are Communists, and have proved it time and again. They may not be exactly like the Russian Communists but they share a common belief in a supranational creed called Communism, and I do not doubt that the leaders in China now will try to make China Communist. Leaders nearly always fail in the end, however, unless they follow the people while they command. Germany was small and Hitler had no great task to shape the Germans to his will, and yet even he had to seek out their private prejudices and coax and cajole them before he was able finally to establish his power over them in the absolute.

But China is not Germany. China is a vast territory of people who are still as difficult to shape as the proverbial tray of sand, which Sun Yat-sen once called them in high impatience. They have allowed the Communists to come in, not because they have any notion of becoming wholesale Communists, but because they have given up hope of President Chiang Kai-shek. They gave him twenty years and he was the same man at the end of it that he was when he came in. No one has ever controlled the Chinese people unless they wanted to be controlled, which has never been. We Americans are disciplined by our politicians, by our police, and by our employers. The Chinese knows no such authority. Compared to the American he is a wild man for freedom, though not on the surface. China is so big that if a man does not like what he has he can always go away a few hundred miles or a couple of thousand. There is no reciprocity act between provinces. Police do not exist in most places. Moreover, the Chinese are organized in a score of private ways of their own against any force which they do not like. Clan unites with clan, secret societies have existed for thousands of years, provincial bonds are strong, trade brotherhoods are as effective as unions, and all this underneath apparent disorder and lack of organization. To the Chinese, Mao Tse-tung's orations are no more to be believed than those of any warlord. That he is a Communist to them is incidental.

It is equally a myth to believe that all those who now proceed under the Communist banner are evil men. We Americans love our myths, we cling to easy classifications of human beings. To be this is to be good, to be that is to be bad. Much as I hold in horror the Ku Klux Klan, I do not doubt that there are good and honest men in it, for reasons of their own. I do not doubt that knights of old thought they were the saviors of society, whereas, knowing modern knights, I am sure they were a nuisance to all hardworking, practical people. If any new government is to exist in China, it will have to shape itself to the hardworking practical people who are most of the population in China. No one discounts more thoroughly than they do windy orations, whether from Nationalists or Communists; no one will weigh more profoundly the actual accomplishments of either side, before commitment. The sort of ecstasy into which the German people seem to have fallen before a man in a uniform, shouting among flags, is impossible to a people as long sane as the Chinese. What is now going on in China gives us not yet the slightest inkling of the shape of things to come, there or in Asia as a whole.

I suppose I might connect this with another myth which is that since the Chinese are, for the most part, illiterate they are therefore ignorant. Actually, there is surprisingly little connection between illiteracy and ignorance. I learned this in my forty years in China, from many friends who, though illiterate, were wise and sophisticated. I learned it again in my own country, where I have found literacy and ignorance in frequent combination. Knowing how to read does not mean that one reads or even thinks. Wisdom is the essential element of civilization and of wisdom the Chinese have much. Nor has civilization anything to do with how one bathes or with kitchen gadgets. The proof of civilization is the type of average person it produces in any given country, and in China the type is high. Everyone should, of course, as a common right, be taught to read and write, so that he may have his own access to the body of the world's knowledge, a right especially important now, so that he may be in the stream of world communication. Science with its gifts of health and conveniences is shut away from those who cannot read. One of the Chinese people's grudges against the Nationalist government has been that it did not provide means for the people to learn to read. Schools were established, it is true, with amazing speed, but they were academic places for the young. In spite of their astounding number they were still not enough to provide education for more than about twenty-five percent of China's young. What President Chiang Kai-shek should have done and what Madame Chiang Kai-shek could have helped him to do, with her knowledge of American democracy, was to establish everywhere people's schools, after the model designed and tested by the Mass Education Movement. Had this been done at once, immediately after 1927, the Nationalists might have been in complete power today. Instead, the whole educational emphasis was on the young student and on higher education, natural perhaps in the great shortage of teachers, but still wrong when mass education was the essential. The same failure is to be seen today in the efforts of UNESCO. It comes from ignorance of peoples and a lack of realization of their immediate and demanding needs.

The profound civilization of the Chinese has been taught by one generation to another and not a little of this achievement is due to Chinese women and the extraordinary place of power that they have long had in Chinese society. I arrive at still another American myth, which is that Chinese women have been much suppressed. Nothing could be farther from the truth. The extraordinary balance in the Chinese individual comes from the wise equality of such differing persons as the man and the woman. Women are, of course, powerful in any society, by fair means or foul, but in China the means has been fair enough, in comparison to that even in the West. I do not know how much of the peculiar position of our Western women has been due to the myth of Adam's rib, as described in the Hebrew Old Testament. It is an obstacle almost insuperable for women to be told, and in a certain era even compelled to believe, that their origin was a mere male rib, and certainly very bad for men to have such a conception. The Chinese creative myth is not so fantastic. There the male and female principle was developed in equal power, with separate functions but equally important. The yang and yin circle perfectly expresses this concept. Thus the Chinese woman has grown up within a sphere socially as concrete and as respected as the man's, and not more circumscribed except in the field of romance, which the Chinese quite accurately comprehend is not as essential to woman as to man. The result has been a female creature much more balanced and less bumptious than the one who is the product of the rib.

There is one more myth, very old and cobwebby indeed. It is that the Chinese are mysterious and inscrutable. Actually, they are the least mysterious and inscrutable of peoples. They are so thoroughly integrated into their civilization and its customs that any foreigner in dealing with them has only to familiarize himself with Chinese civilization and its customs and he will be able to understand the average Chinese and will know what to expect of him under given conditions. The Chinese, actually, is far more predictable and understandable than the average American, for the American acts on individual impulse and the Chinese does not. We have often failed in our dealings with the Chinese because we have not taken the trouble first to understand their civilization and their customs. Chinese before coming to America usually take a good deal of pains to learn as much as they can about us, and they can at least meet a handshake and a smile in a suitable manner, although the handshake is not natural to them. But we Americans tend to hurry to other peoples without previous preparation, not knowing, for example, that while a smile and open friendliness are pleasant to us, in some countries they are an insult, and there the proper behavior to a stranger is solemnity and no physical touch.

Be that as it may, I can only beg that we cast aside forever the myth that the Chinese is mysterious and inscrutable. On the contrary, he is plain, practical, even literal-minded, and certainly very human, under the manners which he has developed through his own centuries.

I have often wondered as I have wandered about my own country in these latter years, why it is that we so readily discard a building that is outmoded and yet cling to an idea long ago obsolete. In cities I see fine and handsome buildings, which in older countries would become monuments of a past age, destroyed to make way for new buildings that will service better the present moment. I wish I could see the same ruthlessness applied to our mental structures of myth. Our national thinking, particularly on international matters, progresses slowly. Perhaps this is because we tinker at it rather than rebuild. Yet the recent tempo quickens. President Truman's Point Four program may prove revolutionary, not, I hasten to say, in the Communist sense, but in the good American sense of scrapping what is no longer sufficient for the times. We shall have to wait and see, at that.

17

What the Peoples of Asia Want

There NEVER WAS a time when history was more important than it is now. Some Americans are inclined to think that everything now happening to us is accidental, and undeserved. It is true, in a sense, that we do not deserve all that we are now enduring, but nothing that is happening is accidental. All is in the inevitable sequence of history. Everything that is happening at this moment in Korea and everywhere else in Asia is a direct result of what has gone before. If you haven't recently read history, not in the day-by-day assignments of students in high schools and colleges, but in the broad sweep of following the peoples of the world in the long reaches of human life, then I pray that you do so now because you cannot possibly understand our present, or foretell our future, unless you understand that what is happening to us at the moment is the result of history—past history in the hundreds of years gone by, and immediate history of the present since the second world war.

Speech before the Chicago Council on Foreign Relations, April 5, 1951.

I speak as an American, because I am an American. I am interested in America, not only because it is my country, but because at this moment in history we are the strategic center of the world. Whether we would be or not, we are.

It is very important, therefore, for us as Americans, before we approach the peoples of Asia, to realize and to accept the fact that we are, for a moment, I hope and trust, only, the most hated people in the world. Every American when he hears that said must have a sense of injustice done him, because above all peoples we have been generous. We have sent men and women from our country for many years as missionaries, to perform good works. We have given with goodwill to the peoples of Asia, and particularly to China. It may seem well-nigh incredible to you, as indeed it does to me, that we should be, and are now, distrusted.

What are the reasons for this attitude toward us of the peoples of Asia? We ought to be able to understand them with our history of freedom and independence. I think we would understand them, and they would understand us (for their understanding of us is just as little as our knowledge and understanding of them), I think that we could come together with mutual benefit, if we examined the barrier that is between us.

The barrier that is between us is a psychological one. It lies in the fact that what is realism for the peoples of Asia is not realism for us. It is quite natural in a people like ourselves, who have lived two thousand years of work and achievement within the space only of some two hundred years, that we should think of realism in terms of practical

achievement. Cities built, industries set up and going as
no industries do anywhere in the world, the tremendous
civilization today that is typically American has been built
in less than three centuries. It is not all material civilization.
I am not one of those who believes that all spiritual life
is in the East. I find among our own American people very
definite spiritual and mental values of which the people of
Asia are totally ignorant, as we are ignorant of them.

For the people in Asia, however, realism means something else, primarily. They value material achievement.
They would like to live without fear of starvation, in houses
sanitary and modern. But they do not express *themselves*
in these ways. They value good human relations, for example, and what we call peace of mind, more even than
bridges and railroads and humming factories. For them
realism is expressed psychologically, let us say. Our approach, therefore, to the people of Asia must be psychological just as their approach to us, to be sure, must be in
terms of objective things and achievements. They are beginning to understand this. But we have not learned to
understand that the peoples of Asia call realism that which
we call the intangibles. But they do, and we have to get
ourselves over that hump of not comprehending before we
can find the rapport which will bring us together in a new
way.

We must find this new comprehension because the peoples
of Asia do not want us on the old terms. They do not want
us anymore on the terms of missionaries bringing an exclusive gospel to them. They do not want us on terms of

business in which we own fifty-one percent. They want us on terms of complete equality. And we will not be able to get that equality, and they will not accept us and therefore we cannot accept them, for acceptance must be mutual, until we understand the state of mind that we each have in our separate sides of the world.

Now, from history, and I must refer again and again to history, we must realize that past centuries in Asia are working against us now. We Americans are actually the most innocent of all peoples in regard to Asia. We never had an empire there, we never planned an empire there, we do not plan an empire now. The more I know Americans, the more I realize that we are not empire-minded people. We cannot, perhaps, concentrate long enough to build an empire. We have not the endless patience for it. We have not the will to dominate. We would get chummy with the people, and you cannot get chummy if you are an empire builder. The more I know of my people the more I know that we are not the stuff of which the past was made—we are the stuff of which the future may be made.

Nevertheless, we have inherited the past. We must not forget that the experience of Asia with the white man from Europe has been an unfortunate one. Nearly every country in Asia was colonial or semicolonial. When I was a child I grew up beside the Yangtze River, and I used to see the American ships, too, with the English and the French and the Germans and Japanese, sailing up and down interior waters of China. We did not belong in that company. We never fought opium wars. We never seized land or asked for concessions. But we did come in like the tail after the dog. We took advantage of what others had won. When special rights were given, we said rather apologetically that we wanted them, too. The peoples of Asia remember this. We clung to the Philippine Islands longer than the Filipinos thought we would, when we fought side by side with them against the tyranny of Spain. We did, after decades, give them their independence, even as England, with magnificent statesmanship, gave up India in the old sense and won back into the English Commonwealth a new India, loyal and friendly.

Three hundred years of unhappy tradition remain in the permanent memory of Asia. All the things you have heard about white domination there are true, and many of which you have not heard. Now it is we who inherit that unhappy past, not the English, not the French, not the Germans, not the Portuguese, not the Spanish, not the Dutch. Their day is over and Asians know it. But they are still afraid of white people and they are afraid of us. We are young, strong, greedy, they fear, for power, as other white peoples have been. We have not made them believe that we are not empire builders. They cannot believe that any white people are not empire builders. It is our task to convince them that we are not.

How is it that we have not been able to do so? Since the end of the second world war the unhappy fact that the Americans representing us in all the countries of occupation have been military men has tended to deepen their fear of us. They want to trade with us, but they are afraid even to trade. They remember that in the past empire began with trade. We shall have to devise a way which will make them believe in us. We shall have to be honest about ourselves because we cannot fool the peoples of Asia. They are far older than we are and they knew all the tricks before our great-grandparents were born. We must convince them that our way of trading is not the beginning of an empire. For there is reason in their fear.

England went first into India as a trader, not as a conqueror, not as an invader, and stayed three hundred years.

Asians are afraid, too, because we have entered Asia with militarism. I am not a pacifist. I believe that war is like any other disease. If we do not create the atmosphere in which germs die, we must face the disease when it attacks. I feel that it was a great misfortune for us, for example, that we had to have military occupation in Japan and in Germany. It would have been a wiser example of democracy to have set up civilian occupations with the military only as police. Had we been able to make the chief in command a civilian, we would not have built upon the distrust and fear psychologically found in all the people of Asia.

There has been historically a difference in the attitudes of the people of Asia and of ourselves toward military men. We make heroes of military men; Asia does not. This difference explains the rather pathetic sight that is so often seen in Indo-China of old warlords who have been great soldiers in their way, who, when they get old, do not want to be remembered as soldiers. Some of them even try to write poetry. It is always very bad poetry. No one can write poetry when nothing in the life before has been poetical. But it is because the people of the East value their poets, their writers, and their saints, that sometimes a soldier tries to forget he has been a soldier.

It has not been so in our country. Some of our most long-remembered people have been military men. We have given an honor to the soldier which is entirely alien and foreign to the man of Asia, who in China at least five hundred years before Christ decided that good men must not be made into soldiers. They take as soldiers only the men of little account just as one does not take good iron to make into nails. It is just scrap iron that makes nails. Thus there was not the slightest protest during the last war when Chiang Kai-shek decided that no college men were to risk being killed on the battlefield because the nation needed them, not only for the development of China, but for the fathers of children to be born. It is very interesting to see the comment in our present newspapers upon that very same subject. It indicates, perhaps, a slight change even in our own attitude that it can be considered that we should save the lives of what presumably are our most promising young men for the safety of the nation and for future fathers. We are beginning to approach something that the Asians have learned.

In Chinese society the soldier was called a destructive force, one who never produced but would only destroy. Yet it was more than that. It was a profound disbelief in force itself—physical force, a conviction that force does not win, finally. This was true throughout Chinese history and Indian history, for every invader was in the end overwhelmed by

271

the superior civilization which he met. In history that country wins which has the superior civilization. It does not matter if military victories have been won; if the incoming civilization is not better than the one it meets, the invader will fall, and did fall.

So far we have not convinced the man of Asia of our superior civilization. He has seen our soldiers, and he has seem them under trying circumstances; he has not, under the circumstances, seen our American men at their best. It is not difficult to reason that some of our problems of today are the result of the impact of our armed forces upon the peoples of Asia, who never knew us before. We have not been able to overcome that impact as yet, by anything that we have said or done. They are not convinced that we are worthy of their respect.

What do they respect in a human being? The first respect of the man of Asia, in spite of his over-high rate of illiteracy, is for the truly educated person. He respects, next, in spite of some lack of integrity among his own average people, the person of integrity. Asians value sincerity, even though they have the most formal courtesy in the world, which includes a great deal of courteous lying. They know when they lie; they do not know when we lie, and that is disturbing. The primary reason for Gandhi's ability to hold his people was his utter sincerity. It would have been very easy for him to have lost his people. Americans have often wondered why it was that when Gandhi went to London he took his goat along and wore his little sheet, when in the old days he was perfectly accustomed to wearing Western morning clothes and a top hat. Gandhi remained Indian in order that he could hold his people. They would have doubted his sincerity if, when he went to Buckingham Palace, he ate roast beef and wore a top hat and morning clothes. But when he went and sat beside the king, and they saw pictures of him sitting beside the king, with his little sheet wrapped around him, and all but heard the "baa" of his goat outside, they knew that Gandhi was sincerely their own. Even though many of them found it difficult to follow Gandhi— he was really too saintly for them—there was something extremely wise and statesmanlike in his saintliness because only a saint, and a real saint, could hold his people.

Now we have not that demand for utter sincerity. We do not like dishonesty. We look at the politicians and we accept a certain amount of it as the Chinese do, and yet even the Chinese, who are accustomed to much human nature, thousands of years of it, and whose moral standards are comfortable, let us say, demand a sincerity which we have got to learn how to present to them.

Another reason why it is unfortunate that military men have to represent us is their attitude toward life. It was poor statesmanship that lost us, I am sure, still more Asian friends, when in Korea our operation was called "Operation Killer." The name was stupid and it showed a lack of knowledge of the mind of Asia. It is stupid for our radio commentators to say, again for example, upon that occasion, that we made the greatest bayonet attack in Korea that has been made since the Civil War. We killed more men by cold steel, it was announced, than in any war since the

Civil War. Perhaps we did, but we should have kept quiet about it, because the announcement lost us what we cannot afford to lose—the mind of the man of Asia. He has been taught by his religion not to kill. He does not like to kill. He will let people linger along, let animals just linger along, in order not to violate his religious principles against the act of taking life. He will let cows in India die a lingering death; he will not kill a fly even when he ought because he believes in the sacredness of life. And he thinks that we do not.

Now there is something irreconcilable here. It is not really irreconcilable, but until we can fathom how the man of Asia feels, we must not go around talking about "Operation Killer." If the diplomats sometimes turn a military victory into defeat, I assure you that sometimes the military lose a victory too, often by the way they speak and act.

And then, of course, what most deeply moves the man of Asia is the instinctive attitude of the white man toward him. We are kind enough to the people of Asia in this country. They have nothing to complain of, perhaps, except that they have not quite as many legal rights as we might have given them. But they divine in us, with that extraordinary third sense which old peoples have, that we do not truly consider Asians our equals, as human beings. He is right. We do not, and we cannot come into good relationship with Asia until we truly root out of us the consciousness of superiority. You know what I mean. Even though the average American enjoys a man from Asia, is enchanted with his conversation, he cannot deny that there is hidden deep

274

in it the consciousness of his own superiority. The Asian feels it.

And of course he looks at Washington. I suppose Washington has done us more damage than can be repaired—our national capital, where a man of color comes and cannot get into a restaurant or into a hotel. There's nothing that we do there that is not known in Asia. I dare say, the people of Asia know more of what happens in our South and in Washington than you and I do. Many a time I have found in Asian papers facts that I did not know, though I live only a few hours from Washington. I shall not speak of the South. We have to give the South its own time. But it is a matter of national importance that we correct the situation in Washington, our national capital, which has become, in a sense, a world capital.

Past history in Asia has been against us. Today we almost alone bear the burden of being the white man in a world most of whose peoples fear and distrust the white man. We have done nothing to lighten the burden since the end of the war. Instead, we made it more heavy, beginning in San Francisco, when, with all of Asia looking up to us, Mr. Stettinius said that we would not concern ourselves with the freedom of colonial people. And that was the beginning of our losing Asia to Communism, for above all else, Asia was determined to be free. Idealism is a reality to the man of Asia. He has to have it. He quite understands our not living up to all our ideals, but he does not understand *announcing* that we are not going to live up to them. And that was the blow.

We must not forget that quite without our will and wish, a sort of an ideal has been built up about America and the Americans everywhere in the world. Our forefathers, with such tremendous vitality, designed a government and a theory of pure idealism. Man cannot live without idealism in Asia. He does not respond even to the impulse of self-interest. We may find this hard to believe, but if we are to reach the peoples of Asia we must believe in ideals, and in *announced* ideals. These people can accept a little hypocrisy more easily than they can announced self-interest, because they have had religion as a spiritual reality, if not a material one, for so long.

In China the people have built their idealism around human relationships. The educated man does not use force; the educated man does not lose his temper; the superior person does not curse and swear. Confucius said these words five hundred years before Christ lived. "The superior man blames himself; the inferior man blames others." A whole nation of people has developed in this atmosphere. So that actually a Chinese of upper class does not lose his temper. He may like to, but he is ashamed to because he would disgrace himself and his family if he did so. That is a kind of practical idealism, too.

Now, what shall we do about this difference between Asian peoples and us—that we call realism two different things? We must understand the idealism on both sides— what is real to us, what is real to them. We must convey to them what it is that we believe in; we must respect their ideals. We must blame ourselves, if we would not have them think us inferior for blaming others. Let me take Korea as an example.

We have lost much in Korea. Of course the people of Korea are the supreme losers; they have nothing left. Their little country hangs from the south of Asia, south of Russia, as Florida hangs on our southern border, and it is so raked and scraped by our bombs and warfare that what was a country green and fair has become a desert. I said to a man in Korea the other day, "Do the people think it is the United States or the United Nations fighting in your country?" He was very careful before he answered me. He said, "Let us say that we call it the United Nations fighting there, but the United States is the energy." And that's what causes my fear that when this cruel time is over, they will forget why we were there, if they know now. They will forget why we were there, but they will only look at their ruined cities, and they will tell what children they have left, "The Americans did this. Why? We don't know. Why did they fight here? We don't know. What were they fighting about? We don't know."

I don't think they do know.

And yet they will remember that all they have ever wanted is a united country. It does not matter much to them, now, perhaps, under what it is united, because they do not care about government and theories as much as we do. The peoples of Asia have national unities so deep in history that they are far less dependent on political unity than we are. To live so many thousands of years upon a piece of earth that all the people are alike, of one skin and color, and all human ways of living are shared in common form, is to make the changes of government unimportant, and political theories and ideologies ephemeral. We whose roots in history are still so shallow must cling to a unifying theory, a permeating principle. Thus, for example, in Indo-China we have fought a certain man because he was Communist. Indo-Chinese did not care that their leader, Ho Chi Minh, was Communist; they cared only that he said he wanted to free his people. Freedom the people of Asia want above all else, and they follow those who promise freedom from colonial rule. But we, who have loved freedom for ourselves, opposed Ho Chi Minh because he was a Communist. We stood for Bao Dai, the French puppet, because he was against Ho Chi Minh. Thus he stood, in the minds of the Indo-Chinese, for empire, and history was against us once more. So the people opposed those whom we supported, whom we did not really approve, and this confusion came about because we have not understood where the realistic idealism of the people lay.

What shall we do in Korea? Well, if we are realistic about Korea, then we have to realize that Korea can never belong to what we call "our side." Never! It cannot even if we win a military victory there. Would we, for example, tolerate Soviet Russia in Mexico? Korea is as close to Russia and China as Mexico is to us. Neither country will endure a government in Korea that is anti-Communist and pro-American. Our own realistic common sense, taking into consideration these feelings of the present Asia, will wish to make Korea a neutral country, under the guardianship of the United Nations. We cannot think only of what we want. We must consider what is possible, in view of the people of Korea. In the guardianship of the United Nations, men of Asia should be the most important, not we, not England, not Europeans, but men of Asia. In every possible way we must neutralize Korea politically and rehabilitate it materially. We have destroyed the lovely Korea that it was. For whatever reason we did it, it is gone. We shall have to build it again with new improvements. We cannot make it the beautiful old Korea, with all its history, but we can at least make it a country where people are healthy, a place where children have the chance of an education. We can help to revive the old Korean culture.

Now, one last thing. The peoples of Asia want independence above all else. And that means independence of us, as well as of empire. Next they want economic help—not relief, but help, and they do not want it from us alone. They want it from the United Nations. Our status now is such that they would profoundly distrust help if it came only from us. Our Point Four program will be useful, frankly, only if it is administered as part of very large scale contribution from the United Nations. We have failed the people of Asia and ourselves by not making the United Nations a success. Yes, we have done our share toward destroying the United Nations. But today we need the United Nations for ourselves. It is for our own sakes that we must rehabilitate the peoples of Asia. We cannot help the history of the past, but we can shape the history of the future. We can move into a new era of common sense, the era of the world view. In this era we will understand at last that peoples need not starve, for there is food enough for all, if wisely administered. There is health for all, if the means of health are wisely administered. It is possible to do away with ignorance and fear, everywhere in the world. The means for such wisdom lie in our total support of the United Nations administrations of World Food, World Health, World Education. This is the real work of the United Nations, necessary if the world's peoples are to be made free for democracy. We have not yet moved into that era. Many of our citizens have, but our government has not. Let us remember that our government is our servant, and not our master.

Now, I will close by repeating the words of Confucius, "The superior man blames himself." Let us not talk about the failures of another people. "The superior man blames himself; the inferior man blames others." With that attitude let us look at our times and see what we can do.

There is no need to be discouraged, because we have infinite resources within ourselves for human understanding as well as for material achievement. I find everywhere in America a splendid spirit, that when people know, they move to action. But the responsibility to know lies very heavily indeed upon us all.

18

China Today

ABRUPTLY I CEASED writing about China after 1951. Searching my files for this collection of speeches and essays about the country and the people I knew so well, apparently I suddenly felt I knew them no longer. There was change, and the change silenced my voice and stilled my pen. The change was of course the fact that what I had foreseen for so many years had finally happened. The Communists came in, the Communists took over. It was to be presumed as early as 1911, when the young revolutionists, most of them the graduates of Christian missionary schools, overthrew the ancient and traditional government and endeavored to replace it with a republic, founded hopefully upon the American system. This overthrow could not possibly have been accomplished had it not coincided time-wise with the decline of the Manchu dynasty, ending finally with the death of the old empress, Tzu Hsi, in 1908.

A feeble effort was made to replace her with an heir too young to rule, too remote to command the respect of the people, but the impetuous young rebels exiled him and took command.

In spite of their enthusiasm and strivings, under the dedicated leadership of Sun Yat-sen, however, they found it impossible to establish a government. In the first place, they did not know how. In the second place, they had no army. In the third place, they had no money. For ten years they struggled. Meanwhile their Russian counterparts to the north were more successful. The revolution of 1917 established a Communist government in Russia, and with success the Russian leaders, observing with sympathy and perhaps with something more, the struggles of the Chinese revolutionists, offered their help, at least in the way of advice.

In desperation Sun Yat-sen accepted, since his pleas to Western governments had brought no response. At the same time he tried to make it clear that he did not believe that Communism would be suitable for his own people. He did, however, ask help in forming an army. I was living in China during those years, and with concern I saw Russian Communist "advisers" stream into China to "advise" not only on how to form an army, set up a military academy, but also take over a country. By 1921 the Communist Party was formally recognized as part of the Chinese political scene and something called the Second Revolution was set up, its center in the Whampoa Military Academy in Canton in the southern province of Kwangtung, under the military leadership of a young man named Chiang Kai-shek, who had been sent to Soviet Russia for a brief period of military education.

Of course all Westerners living in China at the time, myself among them, hoped and believed that the Chinese would be Chinese first, not Communists, and that we had nothing to fear. We had grown accustomed to wars and political strife, and could not imagine the individualistic Chinese becoming Communist. In this belief we were encouraged by Sun Yat-sen himself and had he lived, our faith might have been justified, and history have been very different indeed. Unfortunately he was seized with cancer of the liver and died in 1925. After his death we continued to believe in Chinese human nature. We simply could not think that the Chinese people, so intelligent, so individualistic, would behave as the Russian people had. When Chiang Kai-shek himself turned against Communism in 1927 and set up his own government, the Nationalist Republic of China, we felt our faith was justified.

Faith, however, was not enough. There were practical problems to be attacked and attacked without delay. Basic was the problem of the land. Over the centuries the land had been divided and subdivided, generation after generation, until the average farm, especially north of the Yangtze River, was little more than two acres. This was not enough to feed an average family. Moreover, too much land was in the hands of a few well-to-do peasants and other landlords. Taxes were volatile and imposed by temporary or local rulers. The Communists were promising immediate land

283

reforms as soon as they were able to seize power. Delay was only because Chiang Kai-shek had defected. The struggle for power would continue, the Communists declared. Meanwhile the peasants waited to see who the conqueror would be. The period of waiting was to cover ten years, those between 1928 and 1937. By the end of that period the Japanese were the enemy.

It must not be supposed that Americans then living in China had remained ignorant of the important issue of the land and the peasants. There were hundreds of these Americans, mainly missionaries, without political power or influence, and working always with limited funds. They knew the plight of the peasants, however, and knew that eighty-five percent of China's population were peasants. In Chinese history revolution always began with desperate peasants. Yet it is not to be supposed that all Americans knew Chinese history well enough to realize its meaning in this regard. Some Americans realized it, however, and so did some—a very few—Chinese intellectuals. They had a brief respite in point of time, but how brief they did not realize. When Chiang Kai-shek repudiated Communism and set up his new Nationalist government, they endeavored to begin a rural reconstruction which would at least initiate some improvement in the lot of the peasant. This at first took the form of literacy. If the peasant could be taught to read, it was argued, a technique could be provided for his self-enlightenment. Missionaries, however, were divided even on this procedure. The more evangelical-minded felt that soul-saving was more important and therefore more immediate than knowing how to read. Others felt that if a peasant could read the Scriptures his soul might be saved thereby.

While this argument was in process, a few Chinese intellectuals themselves undertook the task of rural reconstruction. Notable among them was the Mass Education Movement of Dr. James Yen. Of his work I have written in my brief book *Tell the People,* and I need not recapitulate here, except to say that of all efforts to improve the life of the peasant in China, his was the most successful. Beginning at first simply with a literacy movement, Dr. Yen was practical enough to move himself and his family and later his staff to a typical small village in north China and learn at first hand what was needed. He found that merely being able to read was not enough. A literature had to be created which could be of practical use to peasants. Moreover, there were the problems of health, which demanded better food, which meant crop improvement, and sanitation. Taxation was an exorbitant burden to be relieved only by better government. Self-government then was essential for the village. By the time Dr. Yen's program was defined by practice, it had a four-fold purpose, involving the entire life of the peasants.

Similar projects were planned and to some degree executed by a few other men, both Chinese and American, in other places. All were projects of gradualism, however, and there was no time for gradualism. Radical and immediate reforms for the peasants were necessary if they were not to turn to the Communists. For a time the Communist cause seemed to falter. The Communists lost several important battles with Chiang and were in retreat when Mao Tse-tung, then already a Communist but in seclusion because of his disagreement with Russian Communists who disregarded the peasants and placed their confidence in a so-called proletariat, came out of hiding and, reminding the Chinese Communists that revolution in China always began among the peasants, led the movement to gain the support of peasantry. In this he was inadvertently aided by the fact that Chiang Kai-shek ordered all Russians to leave China at once.

But Chiang Kai-shek had his own problems. He was a soldier and had only a soldier's education. He was not an intellectual, nor a theoretician. His heroes in Chinese history were the third-century strategist Liang Chia-ko, and Tseng Kuo-fan, of the last century, who had suppressed all Chinese rebellion against the Manchu rulers. Moreover, Chiang was a provincial. He had never been in the West, or anywhere else, except for his military education in Japan and a brief indoctrination period in Soviet Russia. Courage, sincerity, asceticism, personal loyalty—these were his ideals as a military man—good ideals perhaps, but not sufficient in themselves for the perilous times in which he lived, times in which he must question the loyalty of every person about him. Nevertheless, he represented the only point of stability in that period, and to him every man of ability looked for opportunity to serve. Unfortunately Chiang's suspicious nature, his own limited experience, drove away from him many able and imaginative men who might have saved his government. He trusted only his own family and a few

military associates. Brilliant men such as the rejected intellectual Hu Han-min, and Wang Ching-wei, whose bril-
liance and ambition were so frustrated that he died a Japanese puppet, were lost to the regime as later were Li Tsung-
ren and K. C. Wu, among others. By 1951 Chiang became a
lonely man with no friends.

Yet he had his goals. He was proud and he was determined upon national dignity. His real reason for ridding
his people of Russians was his indignation at the authority
they were assuming, as years later he was to reject General
Joseph Stilwell for the same reason. It was for this same
reason, too, that Chiang insisted through his government
on a revision of the infamous Unequal Treaties. By 1933
the Chinese had regained control over their tariffs, over the
Salt Revenue Administration, the Post Office System, the
Maritime Custom Service. By 1937 the thirty-three foreign
territorial concessions had been reduced to thirteen. In
short, great progress was being made by a proud ruler to
restore his country's sovereign rights. True, there had to
be certain efforts made to meet the demands of modern law
and the Nationalist government therefore devised a new
law code and system of law courts, which Chiang himself
had to learn. He could no longer resort, for example, to
executing men who disagreed with him. At best he could
only imprison them and in time not even that.

The next reform was to establish economic stability, a
difficult task in view of the immense foreign debts. T. V.
Soong, Chiang Kai-shek's Harvard-trained brother-in-law,
established a planning board for economic development

under the advisorship for the League of Nations. Under its guidance, road construction, railroads, and general communication systems were planned and in process. Also some effort was made to reduce the outrageously heavy land rents for peasants. But Chiang remained a soldier at heart and military expenditures always came first. Some excuse may be made for this, since Chiang Kai-shek did indeed face three enemies, or at least their threats: the Communists against whom he had actively fought until they were confined to the northwest; the contending warlords who wished to depose him; and the menacing Japanese militarists who wished to attack China before the Nationalist government grew stronger.

The basic weakness then was financial. The Nationalists were never able to raise enough by taxes to pay for economic construction, educational development, and military costs. T. V. Soong resigned in disgust, and the only solution attempted was to borrow from eastern coastal banks at high rates of interest. But this was what had ruined the past government. True, there were new taxes, particularly on the rich, but the rich, unused to such income taxes, simply did not pay them and there was no means of enforcing payment. It was a basic weakness in the Nationalists that they did not—perhaps could not, after centuries of paternalism in government—realize that a good government is a catalyst, developing the capacities of its citizens. At any rate, in spite of imposing paper plans, there were too few practical results, and the last of these plans, the Three-Year Plan, was stopped by the Sino-Japanese War in 1936.

But the greatest lack in the Nationalist movement was an idealism, a theory, a theme, a motif, a dream, whatever one may call it, something to inspire the people, to fire them to action and patriotism, something to make them sing songs and write slogans. There were no heroes, no great men. Even Sun Yat-sen had not been an inspiring figure. Good soul that he was, he was a plodder, not one who, if he were lifted up, would draw all men to him. Confucianism was dead, and there was nothing to replace it. Before anything could be formed, and while the New Life Movement being devised was still only words, Japan had invaded Manchuria in 1931, and the Communists assumed spiritual leadership. Meanwhile the Nationalists had only improved their tactics and their weapons—an advantage, it must be said, for the future war.

The United States had recognized the Nationalist government in 1928. When Japan invaded Manchuria, there was division in Washington but the prevailing opinion was that our interests with Japan were sufficiently important that we should not annoy her. I was living in Nanking at the time and I remember the consternation of my Chinese friends when it became clear that neither the United States nor the League of Nations would protest Japan's seizure of Manchuria.

"But does not the West understand that this will lead inevitably to a world war?" they asked me.

"They do not understand," I said.

It was so clear to us in China and so far away to the Americans, and we felt helpless as we watched the inexorable march of events. True, Secretary of the Treasury Henry Morgenthau, Jr., understood the Chinese point of view and insisted, over the objection of Secretary of State Cordell Hull, on giving China a substantial loan in the spring of 1933. President Roosevelt, too, had a secret sympathy for China.

"Please remember," he wrote in a memorandum to Morgenthau in late December of that year, "that I have a background of a little over a century in China."

He referred, of course, to his family fortune on his mother's side, whose wealth came from the China trade. But Hull and Stanley Hornbeck continued their pro-Japanese convictions, insisting that no further financial assistance should be given to China, that no Americans should be sent as military advisers to the Chinese and that the export of arms to China should be strictly controlled. They said further that China should be forced to stand on its own feet, and that the United States should not take any action unfavorable to Japan. It must be remembered that these were the years of depression in the United States and the public was apathetic.

From this time onward, the atmosphere in China was one of deepening gloom. The Nationalist Party lost the confidence of the Chinese people, and in 1935 the semiannual report from the American Chargé d'Affaires gave a pessimistic résumé. A year later the American Ambassador said that Communism would continue to be an annoyance to the Nationalists unless something were done about land tenure, since the peasants were increasingly angry because the

Nationalists did nothing. He discussed the matter with H. H. Kung, the Nationalist treasurer, but he made no impression.

The same conviction was deepening in the minds of American missionaries, and we find various attempts at rural reconstruction, village improvements, and the like. It was surprising that their efforts were not at least supplemented by the Nationalist government, for Sun Yat-sen, its founder, had from the very first proposed the equalization of land ownership as a primary and necessary reform. Indeed, so stirring had been his appeal that several Chinese, as private citizens, had set up land reforms resembling in many ways the Mass Education Movement of James Yen. None of them was successful, however, and in some instances the impetuous reformers were assassinated by counterrevolutionists. James Yen's work in Tinghsien proceeded with some success as he attacked what he called the four basic weaknesses of Chinese life: "ignorance, poverty, disease and civic disintegration."

While China was living through the tangle of problems the Christian missionary movement gave world-wide Christian support to rural reconstruction, and this in turn and in time was supported in China by the Nationalist government, mainly through the efforts of Madame Chiang Kai-shek. The cooperation was formulated and led by a Congregational missionary, George William Shepherd. He lived in the southern province of Fukien and from there observed, through three successive incursions of the Communists, the profound appeal of their agarian reform program upon the peasants and the inadequacy of the Nationalist and

Christian approach to the same problem. What was needed, he said, was not Bible schools but rural service training institutes which would be Bible schools, and much more. A new field was opening to the Chinese Church, he went on, and men must be trained for these new rural programs. He went so far as to confer secretly with the Chinese Communist officials and found them favorable to some sort of cooperation.

There was real progress during the next few years, and yet all progress was hampered by the problem of land tenure. The Nationalist government seemed unable to arrive at any real reform in the matter of land distribution and all other efforts therefore were only ameliorative. By the middle of 1935 it was obvious that the greatest weakness of the government, and the greatest danger to its continuance, was its neglect of land reform. It had become a government of and for the landowning class and against the peasant. This fact gave the Communists their strongest appeal for the peasants. By 1939 Generalissimo and Madame Chiang Kai-shek discontinued their usual annual contribution to the Christian rural reconstruction work. This was not only because of the government's policy, but also because of the division among missionaries, many of whom still believed their mission was "soul-saving," and not rural reconstruction.

The Rockefeller Foundation made the next effort in the direction of the rural reconstruction work in China by giving substantial grants to projects already in progress. Its contributions brought universities into contact with rural problems, which up to this time they had ignored, and trained a number of young Chinese rural workers and leaders. Yet it, too, ignored the basic problem of the peasants who formed eighty-five percent of China's population —land reform. All later efforts, such as Madame Chiang's New Life Movement, made the same fatal mistake. Gradualism prevailed through every program designed for the better life of the peasant and no basic reform was initiated either by governmental or private efforts, and Communism was making headway by its propaganda of promises to the peasants. A militant, anti-Christian faith was gaining ground, a political agency whose policy was legalized violence, an agency willing to achieve by force the expropriation of lands and equalization of rights for the Chinese peasants. This was the state of the Chinese nation until December 7, 1941, when Japan attacked Pearl Harbor and the United States declared war on the side of China.

Ten years later Y. T. Wu, who as a Christian had once worked in rural reconstruction, made a "Denunciation of American Imperialism" in which he gave at length the Communist accusation against American missionaries and Chinese Christians during the years under Nationalist rule. Reformism such as they attempted, Wu said, was a false front, designed to avoid class struggle and oppose the use of force to overthrow the old and decadent social order. Even James Yen's work, he declared, was basically anti-Communist, although Americans praised this "worthless anti-Communist churchman." From 1935 on, Wu wrote, "I began to comprehend the error of reformism. . . . All of us have been the tools of American cultural aggression, perhaps without being wholly conscious of it."

Of all this and much more I was aware while I lived in China. After I left China permanently in 1933, knowing that Communism would win because of its growing appeal to the peasantry, and knowing, too, not only that I could not live in a Communist-controlled country but also that Chinese Communists would not tolerate Americans who were not Communist, I then devoted my efforts to helping Chinese in the United States not to be deported to Communist China.

There is at present a widespread feeling throughout the United States that we Americans need and want more information about mainland China. A. T. Steele, in his book about China, *The American People and China,* gives the result of many interviews with Americans in various areas of life and business, and they all agree that our press coverage of China is very poor, that we do not know what is going on there from authoritative sources, that information is too scanty for us to put our policies in true perspective, that what we do say is critical and highly colored. It is surprising to discover the number of Americans who have a genuine interest in the Chinese people and who would like to have sound information upon which to base their own opinions. Lacking directive opinions from the people, even the President cannot be expected to be able to formulate new and practical policies toward the China of today. True, it has not been easy and until recently it has been impossible to get reporters in and out of China proper. But one must assume that the news media themselves are also at fault for underestimating the general intelligence of their reading public and the range of its interest. There are, nevertheless, a number of excellent books on the years of Communist rule in China, their information based for the most part on travels and experiences of British and European writers, as well as a few Chinese writers who are in touch with relatives still living in China.

In brief, however, certain events are clear. The war, spreading as it did after the attack on Pearl Harbor, served to bring the Nationalist, Communist, and American forces on Chinese soil. It was a strange but necessary and practical alliance against an invading Japan. Until then the Chinese Communist strategy had been to exploit fully every revolutionary situation. Not only were the peasants in such despair that land reform took precedence in their minds over all else, but the workers in factories formed unions in the 1920's, and these organizations sprang up over the entire country, demanding better pay and working conditions. The trade union movement became a power for strikes and boycotts of foreign trade, particularly the British, and Chiang Kai-shek found it necessary to use the most severe strong-arm methods to put down the leaders. In the spring of 1927, for example, tens of thousands of Chinese workers in factories in Shanghai were killed, and for a time Communism was wiped out of Shanghai, although only for a time. Student unrest, too, had early made itself felt in the nation, for the new schools and provincial universities installed hastily by the Nationalist government were ill housed and ill staffed. The students united frequently with the factory workers, especially against foreign interests in China.

In May, 1928, the Communists gathered themselves together under the leadership of Mao Tse-tung, who had come out of hiding after his separation from the Russian advisers. This disagreement was based on Mao's conviction that Communism in China must develop differently from Communism in Russia, since in China there was no true proletariat as there was in Russia, and the peasants were the real force of the revolution. Nevertheless, by 1930 the Communists in China were all but cowed by Chiang Kai-shek's repressive methods. Even rebellious students were quiet. The Communists, however, were by no means vanquished. In semiretreat they became divided between the peasant leader Mao and a military leader, Li Li-san, a French-trained Communist intellectual. In September, 1930, the split was made definite. Mao and with him Chu Teh, a Communist general, refused to obey Li's orders to recapture the city of Changsha. This meant, in short, that they refused to obey the Central Committee of the Communist Party. The risk they took was great. Would the peasants and workers follow them? They did, for Mao was already the most popular of the Communist leaders. The Central Committee realized that it was Li who must be censured and not Mao, and from then on Mao Tse-tung became the venerated leader of the Chinese Communist movement, and directed its policies. On November 7, 1931, in a little market town in Kiangsi province, the Chinese Soviet Republic was proclaimed and Mao Tse-tung was made its permanent Chairman. On January 6, 1935, he was elected also Chairman of the Communist Party of China.

Meantime Chiang Kai-shek had continued his relentless pursuit and attack of the Communists until at last he drove them into the far northwest. Of the Long March much has been written and the story need not be repeated here. The Communists established themselves in distant Yenan and Chiang Kai-shek turned his attention to matters of government until the threat of immediate attack by Japan gave the Communists a fresh chance. Chiang Kai-shek had given command against the Communists in the northwest to young Marshal Chang Hsüeh-liang, former warlord of Manchuria, now occupied by Japan. The young man dreamed of regaining his lost territory and instead of fighting the Communists he joined them in Sian, then the capital. Alarmed by this defection, Chiang flew to Sian, arriving on December 9, 1936, a day on which a disorderly anti-Japanese demonstration was going on. He commanded an immediate stop to such disorders, and waited at a nearby town. During the night his bodyguard was attacked, and he was compelled to escape through a window and hid in a fox's hole on a nearby mountain, where he was discovered half frozen in the morning and carried to Sian as a prisoner. Nor was he freed until he had promised to turn all his strength to fighting the Japanese and forming a common front with the Communists in order to do so.

Immense enthusiasm overwhelmed the Chinese people

at the news of this union and Party membership rose rapidly as young men joined to fight the common enemy, Japan. They did not, however, try to form a single organization with the Nationalists, as they had in 1924. On September 22, 1937, they made separate appeals to the nation which, however, agreed on the essentials for fighting Japan. The Communists gave to the national army 45,000 men, known as the 8th Route Army, and in return were allowed to travel and recruit in other parts of China.

The traditional army was almost useless in defending China. It was the revolutionary army, skilled in guerrilla warfare, harassing the enemy from the rear while rousing the populace, that proved the more efficacious. In such tactics Mao Tse-tung had long schooled himself, ancient tactics first described in the classic old novel *Shui Hu Chuan,* which during the early thirties I had translated under the English title *All Men Are Brothers,* foreseeing that someday our American men might have to fight in Asia against just such tactics, as indeed they have. I have heard, incidentally, that Mao Tse-tung always kept a copy of *Shui Hu Chuan* in his knapsack and frequently studies it to this day, and I am the more inclined to believe it true, since certain of his strategies exactly reproduce those in this book. At any rate, the zeal and efficiency of the 8th Route Army were such that from 40,000 members of the Party in 1937, the number had risen to 1,200,000 by 1945.

It is doubtful, nevertheless, whether without American help China could have won the war against Japan. The attack on Pearl Harbor therefore was of the greatest significance to China. True, Chiang Kai-shek seemed never to be throwing his full effort against the Japanese, a fact highly irritating to certain American generals, particularly to Stilwell. Chiang was indeed holding back his own forces all during the war for use after the war and the inevitable future struggle with the Communists. But for the time being Americans, Nationalists, and Communists fought side by side against the Japanese armies. After each victory, however, the Americans withdrew their forces to fight elsewhere, and Chiang withdrew his armies prudently. Only the Communists always left behind a holding cell, an important fact to remember, for when Japan capitulated in August, 1945, her forces, scattered over China, were compelled to surrender to the Chinese Communist cells. Not all our American efforts to help Chiang could serve to save China from the Communists, nor was Chiang in any mood to form a coalition government with them. American efforts to make peace failed; civil war began, ending in defeat for the Nationalist armies. On January 1, 1949, Chiang Kai-shek offered to make peace, but Mao Tse-tung, two weeks later, laid down terms so severe that Chiang could not accept them. In May, 1949, the Communist troops marched into Shanghai. Since then, the Chinese have been under strict Communist rule.

Economic and technological progress has been pressed to the utmost by the Communists. Certain steps toward modernization had been taken, it is true, by the Nationalists. For example, the Chinese railroad system had almost doubled since 1929. But R. H. Tawney, the English economist, in 1932, when he was staying in my home in Nanking and writing his seminal book, *Land and Labour in China,* estimated that even if 10,000 miles of railroad were built every year in China, so vast is the country it would take 180 years before China would have a rail network proportionately as adequate as that of Britain. China's present 25,000 miles of railroad can scarcely compare to the 30,000 miles of railroad in France, for example, since France is eighteen times smaller than China. China's mighty rivers and lakes, however, and her canals, make up somewhat for the shortage of railroad.

But the real changes under Communist rule have been social, rather than technological. Peasants were freed from exploitation by landlords, but were compelled to join cooperatives. Land was redistributed, but cooperatives were changed into communes. The most significant result of the communes was the breakup of the ancient family system and the consequent separation of young and old, children and parents, even men and women. China became a vast factory, agricultural and mechanical. In their haste to create a modern industrialized nation, the Chinese sacrificed traditional securities. The experiment of local "backyard blast furnaces" in 1958 was an example of haste and failure. The communes survived, but they became agricultural rather than industrial. Indeed, the whole Chinese society under Communism has tended to become ruralized. Intellectuals, industrialists, landowners have been forced to approach the peasant level rather than the peasant lifted to a higher level. The announced policy of the Communist

government in China is to "understand the peasant problem." Instead of the early haste to become an industrialized
nation the government maintains that "agriculture is the
basic element of the Chinese economy."

It is true that the intellectual and the more or less
educated businessman of old China composed an élite far
too remote from the mass of the peasantry and indeed
tended to scorn the peasant as a being of a lower order.
But the necessity now to persuade the peasants to accept
basic socialist principles means that such ideas must be
adjusted to the very low level of the peasant. The general
backwardness of the peasant has imposed a very heavy
burden on the whole country. Mao Tse-tung has established
the policy, however, that the intellectual and technical élite
are not to separate themselves from the masses. It is a
reform that the old order needed to some degree, for in
the China in which I grew up, the educated, the brilliant, the
creative, the successful financially had no concern for
the manual laborer, the poor, the peasant. Yet I cannot believe that any nation can afford the total loss of the productive ability of the superior mind and talent.

The unity of China today depends upon Mao Tse-tung.
The influence of his personality still holds the country
together, in spite of considerable internecine struggle within
the Party, as old age approaches Mao. The Chinese mainland has, for purposes of efficiency, been divided into six
districts, ruled each by its own bureau since their reorgan-
ization in 1961. Those bureaus are firmly established and
maintain their authority in three ways: first, their leaders

301

represent the Communist Party's Central Committee, as declared in Article 29 of the Party Constitution; second, the chiefs of the regional bureaus are also the commanders of the regional military forces; third, the people of the region tend to give their first loyalty to the leader of their own regional bureau.

Reviewing the trends of past Chinese history, the dispassionate observer is inclined to ask if this regional division under a specific leader does not represent a traditional pattern, into which the Chinese people may fall again after the death of Mao—which cannot be many years hence. For when in the past it became apparent that a dynasty had ended, regional rulers appeared, men of natural capacity to lead the people, and when the emperor died, these regional leaders contended by battle until a final victor appeared, who then established himself, and was accepted by the people, as the first emperor of a new dynasty. Time alone can tell, but the ancient framework is there.

Entirely new, however, is the emphasis on youth. In old China the traditional family system treasured the children, taught them ancient ways, was responsible for their education and welfare and behavior. The breakup of the Chinese family under Communism has created an entirely new class of young people who are under the control of local government, who have grown up, frequently, away from their families, who consider Mao Tse-tung their idol, and the State their family. All Chinese children today, from the age of three, are organized and indoctrinated into Communism. There were supposed to be 50,000,000 of the Child

Vanguards alone wearing their red neckerchiefs. Above them was the Communist Youth Corps, lost in the recent cultural upheaval, but the Vanguards have survived as younger members of the Red Guards.

Under Mao's express direction the children of China have been organized ever since the revolution of 1921–1923. Mao himself set forth the fundamental principles of child training by saying "Juvenile organizations are schools where children learn Communism." The result of this has been the recent development of the young extremists, the Red Guards, who undertook to criticize and reform their elders, and indeed anyone who displeased them. They formed an élite of their own, in many places, violent and uncontrollable, reminding the unprejudiced student of Chinese history of the traditional bureaucrats in the old regime of China's past. So violent did the Red Guards become, under Mao's initial encouragement, that it was finally necessary for the Central Party itself to order a halt to their excesses and to disband them as far as possible.

However critical we Americans must be of this Communist era of China's history, certain encouraging facts emerge, not from Communist propaganda or theory, but from the native ability of the Chinese people themselves and the revivifying effect of any upheaval in their society. This particular upheaval has compelled the Chinese people to think in terms of self-help. For example, there is a shortage of fertilizers in China. The Chinese cannot import chemical fertilizers from abroad. They have, it is true, begun to make their own chemical fertilizers in such plants as the Kirin Chemical Industry Complex, which produces 400,000 tons of synthetic ammonium each year, or the Wuching Chemical Plant in Shanghai. But farmers do not want to depend on chemical fertilizers. Instead they have also developed a cooperative industry of their own in hog manure. There are also small local nitrogen fertilizer industries developing, each producing only a few thousand tons a year, but beneficial to local agriculture. Similarly farmers belonging to People's Communes and using the principles of self-help have not only collected animal manure and helped to build local industry, but they have carried out irrigation projects of some size, and without the aid of modern equipment.

Nor are farmers the only group who are using the principle of self-help. Many of the communes are thinking and working in terms of individual production. Take, for example, the Shanghai Steel Pipe Plant, a typical factory in China today, operating as a semigovernmental concern. It is a small plant with some 360 employees, more or less, but they produce about 250 types of steel pipes. The building is a hovel by Western standards, but production is high. The factory began in 1958 with about twenty artisans of various sorts, all without experience. The government had asked for a certain type of steel pipe, no longer available after the split with the Soviet Union. These workers, the entire staff, sought and found a new method of manufacturing steel pipes and solid-drawn dies for the pipes.

Time and space forbid the repetition of such examples.

What seems evident from available information, however, is that the Chinese people are recovering from the upheaval of a violent revolution and a total disruption of their ancient social patterns. In 1966 Communist China had the largest food and cotton crop recorded during its existence, and industrial production rose by more than twenty percent over the previous year. This recovery is sufficiently advanced so that the natural Chinese good sense, practical ability, and unequalled intelligence are manifesting themselves again. The Chinese are awakening from shock. They have learned from such egregious mistakes as the Great Leap Forward; they are beginning to look to themselves for solutions to their own problems, local and governmental, instead of expecting an ideology to save them.

In short, the true Chinese is emerging once more. What he will do with what he sees when he wakens completely from the dream—or the nightmare—in which he has been living in recent years remains to be guessed at, or seen. But he is awake—that is the fact of supreme importance and cause for hope.